THE WORLD'S GREATEST COLLECTION OF

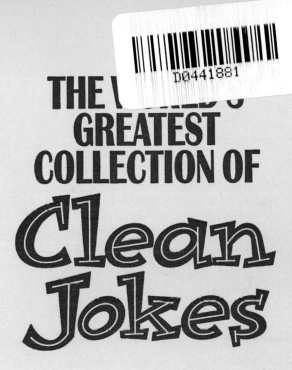

Clean Jokes

Bob Phillips

HARVEST HOUSE PUBLISHERS
Eugene, Oregon 97402

THE WORLD'S GREATEST COLLECTION OF CLEAN JOKES
Copyright © 1998 by Bob Phillips
Published by Harvest House Publishers
Eugene, Oregon 97402

ISBN: 1-56507-987-6

Printed in the United States of America.

03 04 / BC / 10 9 8

Contents

Introduction

As one attempts to write a book, even a joke book, he often encounters periods of depression and a slowing of motivation. During periods of depression, I was spurred on by an important quote designed for writers:

> If you steal from one author, it's plagiarism;
> If you steal from two or three authors, it's literary discernment;
> If you steal from many, it's masterful research.

Joke telling can be a lot of fun. Or it can be a disaster, like the man who told a joke and everyone booed except one man—he was applauding the booing.

If you would like to guarantee disaster in your joke telling, follow these suggestions:

1. Make sure you forget the punch line; sadists enjoy a letdown.

2. Laugh at your own joke and be sure to jab your audience during the process.

3. Tell the same story over if the point is missed. This will assure at least wry smiles.

4. Make sure the story is long enough to lull the dull ones to sleep.

5. Tell the wrong joke to the wrong audience; they'll feel worse than you do.

6. Above all else, don't be yourself because you know you're not humorous, even if you are funny.

If, on the other hand, you would like to have some measure of success in joke telling—ignore these suggestions.

—Bob Phillips

Adam and Eve

At what time of day was Adam born?
A little before Eve.

❖ ❖ ❖

When was radio first mentioned in the Bible?
*When the Lord took a rib from Adam and made a
loudspeaker.*

❖ ❖ ❖

Eve: Adam, do you love me?
Adam: Who else?

❖ ❖ ❖

Adam and Eve were naming the animals of
the earth when along came a rhinoceros.

"What shall we call this one?" Adam asked.
"Let's call it a rhinoceros," said Eve.
"Why?" responded Adam.
"Well, it looks more like a rhinoceros than anything we've named yet!" Eve replied.

✧ ✧ ✧

Teacher: Why was Adam a famous runner?
Student: Because he was first in the human race.

✧ ✧ ✧

Adam was created first . . . to give him a chance to say something.

✧ ✧ ✧

What a good thing Adam had—when he said something he knew nobody had said it before.

✧ ✧ ✧

The first Adam-splitting gave us Eve, a force which men in all ages have never gotten under control.

Airplanes

Passenger: Excuse me. How high is this plane?
Flight Attendant: About 30,000 feet.
Passenger: And how wide is it?

✧ ✧ ✧

The loudspeaker of the big jet clicked on and the captain's voice announced in a clear, even tone: "Now there's no cause for alarm but we felt you should know that for the last three hours we've been flying without the benefit of radio, compass, radar, or navigational beam due to the breakdown of certain key components. This means that we are, in the broad sense of the word, lost and not quite sure in which direction we are heading. I'm sure you'll be glad to know however, that we're making excellent time!"

❖ ❖ ❖

An airliner flew into a violent thunderstorm and was soon swaying and bumping in the sky. One very nervous lady happened to be sitting next to a clergyman and turned to him for comfort.

"Can't you do something?" she demanded.

"I'm sorry, ma'am," said the reverend gently. "I'm in sales, not management."

❖ ❖ ❖

A man is now able to go across the United States in eight hours . . . four hours for flying, and the other four to get to the airport.

❖ ❖ ❖

The airline company was disturbed over a high percentage of accidents and decided to eliminate human errors by building a completely mechanical plane.

"Ladies and gentlemen," came a voice over a loudspeaker on the plane's maiden voyage, "it may interest you to know that you are now traveling in the world's first completely automated plane. Now just sit back and relax because nothing can possibly go wrong . . . go wrong . . . go wrong . . . go wrong . . ."

✧ ✧ ✧

That airplane flight was so rough that the flight attendants poured the food directly into the sick sacks!

✧ ✧ ✧

Pilot: Control tower, what time is it?
Control tower: What airline is this?
Pilot: What difference does that make?
Control tower: If it is United Airlines, it is 6:00 P.M.; if it is TWA, it is 1800 hours; if it is Smogarian Air, the big hand is on the ..."

✧ ✧ ✧

Passenger: Say, this is the worst steak I've ever had. Don't you flight attendants even know how to serve a steak? Bring me another steak right now!
Flight attendant: Will that be to take out?

✧ ✧ ✧

Flight attendant: I am sorry, Mr. Jones, but we left your wife behind in Chicago.
Man: Thank goodness! I thought I was going deaf!

✧ ✧ ✧

Pilot: Pilot to tower ... pilot to tower ... I am 300 miles from land ... 600 feet high and running out of gas ... please instruct ... over.

Tower: Tower to pilot. . . . tower to pilot . . .
repeat after me . . . "Our Father, which art in
heaven . . ."

❖ ❖ ❖

The other day one of those jumbo jets took
off from New York with 400 passengers, then
had to make a forced landing in Newark
because of a hernia.

❖ ❖ ❖

Last week I was flying on a plane and almost
had a heart attack when I noticed a sign on the
door of the pilot's cabin that said "Student
Pilot."

Army and Police

Officer: Soldier, do you have change for a dollar?
Soldier: Sure, buddy.
Officer: That's no way to address an officer.
 Now, let's try that again. Soldier, do you have
 change for a dollar?
Soldier: No, sir!

❖ ❖ ❖

An Army base staff that was planning war
games didn't want to use live ammunition.
Instead they informed the soldiers: "In place of a
rifle, you go, 'Bang, bang.' In place of a knife,
you go, 'Stab, stab.' In place of a hand grenade,
you go, 'Lob, lob.'"

The game was in progress when one of the
soldiers saw one of the enemy. He said, "Bang,
bang," but nothing happened. He ran forward
and shouted, "Stab, stab," but nothing

happened. He ran back and went, "Lob, lob," but nothing happened. Finally he walked up to the enemy and said, "You're not playing fair. I went 'Bang, bang' and 'Stab, stab' and 'Lob, lob' and you haven't fallen dead yet!"

The enemy responded, "Rumble, rumble, I'm a tank."

✧ ✧ ✧

A very new soldier was on sentry duty at the main gate of a military outpost. His orders were clear: No car was to enter unless it had a special sticker on the windshield. A big Army car drove up with a general seated in the back.

The sentry said, "Halt, who goes there?"

The chauffeur, a corporal, said, "General Wheeler."

"I'm sorry, I can't let you through. You've got to have a sticker on the windshield."

The general said, "Drive on."

The sentry said, "Hold it. You really can't come through. I have orders to shoot if you try driving in without a sticker."

The general repeated, "I'm telling you, son, drive on."

The sentry walked up to the rear window and said, "General, I'm new at this. Do I shoot you or the driver?"

❖ ❖ ❖

A blowhard Air Force major was promoted to colonel and received a brand-new office. His first morning behind the desk, an airman knocked on the door and asked to speak to him. The colonel told him to come in. Then, feeling the urge to impress the young airman, the major picked up his phone and said: "Yes, General, thank you. Yes, I will pass that along to the president this afternoon. Yes, goodbye, sir."

Then turning to airman he barked, "And what do you want?"

"Nothing important, sir," said the airman. "I just came to install your telephone."

❖ ❖ ❖

Just before a farm boy had his first parachute jump, his sergeant reminded him, "Count to ten then pull the first rip cord. If it snarls, pull the second rip cord for the auxiliary chute. After you land, our truck will pick you up."

The paratrooper took a deep breath and jumped. He counted to ten and pulled the first cord. Nothing happened. He pulled the second cord. Again, nothing happened. As he careened crazily earthward, he said to himself, *I'll bet that truck won't be there either!*

❖ ❖ ❖

One day a sergeant came into the barracks and asked his men if any of them knew short-hand. The recruits thought it would be easy duty and raised their hands.

"Good," said the sergeant. "They're short-handed in the mess hall!"

❖ ❖ ❖

Bill: My wife just got a ticket for speeding.
Ray: That's nothing! My wife is so bad the police gave her a season ticket.

❖ ❖ ❖

A driver tucked this note under the windshield wiper of his automobile: "I've circled the block for 20 minutes. I'm late for an appointment, and if I don't park here I'll lose my job. 'Forgive us our trespasses.' "

When he came back he found a parking ticket and this note: "I've circled the block for 20 years, and if I don't give you a ticket, I'll lose my job. 'Lead us not into temptation.'"

❖ ❖ ❖

The car stalled at a traffic light as the lights went from red, to green, to yellow, to red, to green, to yellow, to red. Finally a cop came up and asked, "Pardon me, sir, but don't we have any color you like?"

❖ ❖ ❖

"Hello, police department? I've lost my cat and . . ."

"Sorry, sir, that's not a job for the police, we're too busy."

"But you don't understand . . . this is a very intelligent cat. He's almost human. He can practically talk."

"Well, you'd better hang up, sir. He may be trying to phone you right now."

❖ ❖ ❖

"What am I supposed to do with this?" grumbled the motorist as the police clerk handed him a receipt for his traffic fine.

"Keep it," the clerk advised. "When you get four of them, you get a bicycle."

❖ ❖ ❖

Things are so bad in our town that the police department has an unlisted telephone number.

❖ ❖ ❖

The best safety device is a rearview mirror with a cop in it.

❖ ❖ ❖

Officer to a man pacing the sidewalk at 3:00 A.M.:
    What are you doing here?
Gentleman: I forgot my key, officer, and I'm
    waiting for my children to come home and
    let me in.

❖ ❖ ❖

A rookie officer was asked the following
question on his examination paper: "How would
you go about dispersing a crowd?"

He answered: "Take up an offering. That
does it every time."

❖ ❖ ❖

Game warden: Fishing?
Man without a license: No, drowning worms.

❖ ❖ ❖

Stranger: Catch any fish?
Fisherman: Did I! I took 30 out of this stream
    this morning.
Stranger: Do you know who I am? I'm the
    game warden.
Fisherman: Do you know who I am? I'm
    the biggest liar in the country.

❖ ❖ ❖

Judge: Order in this court! I'll have order in
    this court!
Man: I'll have a hamburger with onions!

❖ ❖ ❖

In the traffic court of a large Midwestern city,
a young lady was brought before the judge to
answer for a ticket given her for driving through
a red light. She explained to his honor that she
was a schoolteacher and requested an immediate
disposal of her case so she could get to the
school on time. A wild gleam came into the
judge's eye.

"You're a schoolteacher, eh?" said he.
"Madam, I shall realize my lifelong ambition.
I've waited years to have a schoolteacher in this
court. Sit down at that table and write 'I went
through a red light' 500 times!"

❖ ❖ ❖

Burglar: The police are coming! Quick, jump out
    the window!
Accomplice: But we're on the thirteenth floor!
Burglar: This is not the time to be superstitious.

❖ ❖ ❖

The other day a guy pointed a gun at me
and said, "Stick 'em up and congratulations!"

I asked, "What's the congratulations for?"

He said, "You are now entering a lower tax bracket."

❖ ❖ ❖

A bank robber held up a bank. "Give me all your money," he demanded.

"Here, take the books, too. I'm short 10,000 dollars," replied the teller.

❖ ❖ ❖

"Excuse me for being nervous," the sheriff apologized as he slipped the noose over the condemned man's head. "This is my first hanging."

"Mine too!" replied the criminal.

❖ ❖ ❖

A fellow walked up to me and said, "Stick 'em down."

I said, "You mean stick 'em up?"

He said, "No wonder I haven't made any money."

❖ ❖ ❖

A young soldier, an officer, a little old lady, and an attractive young woman were riding on a train.

Shortly after the train entered a dark tunnel, the passengers heard a kiss, then a loud slap.

The young woman thought: "Isn't that odd, the officer tried to kiss the old lady and not me?"

The old lady thought: "That is a good girl with fine morals."

The officer thought: "That soldier is a smart fellow; he steals a kiss and I get slapped."

The soldier thought: "Perfect. I kiss the back of my hand, clout an officer, and get away with it."

✧ ✧ ✧

A burglar entered the house of a Quaker and proceeded to rob it. The Quaker heard noises, took his shotgun downstairs, and found the burglar. He aimed his gun and said gently: "Friend, I mean thee no harm, but thou standest where I am about to shoot."

✧ ✧ ✧

An FBI agent was talking to a bank teller after the bank was robbed for the third time by the same bandit.

"Did you notice anything special about the man?" he asked.

"Yes, he seems better dressed each time," the teller replied.

4

Bald

If a man is bald in front, he's a thinker. If he's bald in the back, he's a lover. If he's bald in front and back, he thinks he's a lover.

❖ ❖ ❖

"Papa, are you growing taller all the time?"
"No, my child. Why do you ask?"
" 'Cause the top of your head is poking up through your hair."

❖ ❖ ❖

A bald man's retort: "In the beginning God created all men bald. Later He became ashamed of some and covered them with hair."

❖ ❖ ❖

He has wavy hair—it's waving goodbye.

❖ ❖ ❖

He's not bald . . . he just has flesh-colored hair.

❖ ❖ ❖

He's a man of polish . . . mostly around his head.

❖ ❖ ❖

There's one proverb that really depresses him: "Hair today, gone tomorrow."

❖ ❖ ❖

He has less hair to comb, but more face to wash.

❖ ❖ ❖

It's not that he's bald . . . he just has a tall face.

❖ ❖ ❖

There's one thing about baldness . . . it's neat.

❖ ❖ ❖

There's a new remedy on the market for baldness. It's made of alum and persimmon juice. It doesn't grow hair, but it shrinks your head to fit what hair you have.

5

Barbers

I couldn't stand my boy's long hair any longer, so I dragged him with me and ordered, "Give him a crew cut." The barber did just that, and so help me, I found I'd been bringing up somebody else's son!

✧ ✧ ✧

I've got a 16-year-old son who was 6' 3" until he got a haircut. Now he is 5' 8".

✧ ✧ ✧

The customer settled himself and let the barber put the towel around him. Then he told the barber, "Before we start, I know the weather's awful. I don't care who wins the next big fight, and I don't bet on the horse races. I know I'm getting thin on top, but I don't mind. Now get on with it."

"Well, sir, if you don't mind," said the barber, "I'll be able to concentrate better if you don't talk so much!"

✧ ✧ ✧

A man entered a barber shop and said, "I am tired of looking like everyone else! I want a change! Part my hair from ear to ear!"

"Are you sure?"

"Yes!" said the man.

The barber did as he was told and a satisfied customer left the shop.

Three hours passed and the man reentered the shop. "Put it back the way it was," he said.

"What's the matter?" asked the barber. "Are you tired of being a nonconformist already?"

"No," he replied, "I'm tired of people whispering in my nose!"

✧ ✧ ✧

Customer (twice nicked by the barber's razor): Hey, barber, gimme a glass of water.
Barber: What's wrong, sir? Hair in your mouth?
Customer: No, I want to see if my neck leaks.

Bible Quiz

When were automobiles first mentioned in the Bible?
When Elijah went up on high.

❖ ❖ ❖

What simple affliction brought about the death of Samson?
Fallen arches.

❖ ❖ ❖

Who was the most successful physician in the Bible?
Job. He had the most patients.

❖ ❖ ❖

Who was the best financier in the Bible?
Noah. He floated his stock while the whole world was in liquidation.

✧ ✧ ✧

Who is the straightest man in the Bible?
Joseph. Pharaoh made a ruler out of him.

✧ ✧ ✧

Where is tennis mentioned in the Bible?
When Joseph served in Pharaoh's court.

✧ ✧ ✧

What animal took the most baggage into the
ark?
*The elephant. He took his trunk, while the fox and the
rooster only took a brush and comb.*

✧ ✧ ✧

What man in the Bible had no parents?
Joshua, the son of Nun.

✧ ✧ ✧

Who is the smallest man in the Bible?
*Some people believe that it was Zacchaeus. Others
believe it was Nehemiah (Ne-high-miah), or
Bildad, the Shuhite (Shoe-height). But in reality it
was Peter, the disciple. He slept on his watch!*

✧ ✧ ✧

When is baseball mentioned in the Bible?
*When Rebecca walked to the well with the pitcher,
and when the prodigal son made a home run.*

❖ ❖ ❖

When is money first mentioned in the Bible?
When the dove brought the green back to the ark.

❖ ❖ ❖

Who is the most popular actor in the Bible?
Samson. He brought the house down.

❖ ❖ ❖

Do you know how you can tell that David was older than Goliath?
Because David rocked Goliath to sleep!

❖ ❖ ❖

What instructions did Noah give his sons about fishing off the ark?
Go easy on the bait, boys. I only have two worms.

❖ ❖ ❖

Joe: Was there any money on Noah's ark?
Moe: Yes. The duck took a bill, the frog took a green back, and the skunk took a scent.

❖ ❖ ❖

Why didn't they play cards on Noah's ark?
Because Noah sat on the deck.

❖ ❖ ❖

How did Jonah feel when the great fish swallowed him?
Down in the mouth.

When is high finance first mentioned in the
   Bible?
*When Pharaoh's daughter took a little prophet from
   the bulrushes.*

When did Moses sleep with five people in one
   bed?
When he slept with his forefathers.

Teacher: Where was Solomon's temple?
Student: On the side of his head.

Fay: How long did Cain hate his brother?
Ray: As long as he was Abel.

7

Boys and Girls

"When I went out with Fred, I had to slap his face five times."

"Was he that fresh?"

"No! I thought he was dead!"

✧ ✧ ✧

Girl: Did you kiss me when the lights were out?
Boy: No!
Girl: It must have been that fellow over there!
Boy, starting to get up: I'll teach him a thing or two!
Girl: You couldn't teach him a thing!

✧ ✧ ✧

You can't kiss a girl unexpectedly . . . only sooner than she thought you would.

❖ ❖ ❖

"Well, and how are you getting on with your courtship of the banker's daughter?"

"Not so bad. I'm getting some encouragement now."

"Really, is she beginning to smile sweetly at you or something?"

"Not exactly but last night she told me she'd said 'no' for the last time."

On a lonely, moonlit country road the engine coughed and the car came to a halt.

"That's funny," said the young man. "I wonder what that knocking was?"

"Well, I can tell you one thing for sure," the girl answered icily. "It wasn't opportunity."

❖ ❖ ❖

Boy: Why won't you marry me? Is there someone else?
Girl: There must be.

"I just had a date with Siamese twins."
"Did you have a good time?"
"Yes and no."

❖ ❖ ❖

Girl: The man I marry must be as brave as a
    lion, but not forward; as handsome as Apollo,
    but not conceited; as wise as Solomon, but
    meek as a lamb; a man who is kind to every
    woman, but loves only me.
Boy: How lucky we met!

❖ ❖ ❖

"Without you, everything is dark and
dreary. . . . The clouds gather and the wind beats
the rain . . . then comes the warm sun. . . . You
are like a rainbow."
    "Is this a proposal or a weather report?"

Joe: What's so unusual about your girlfriend?
Moe: She chews on her nails.
Joe: Lots of girls chew on their nails.
Moe: Their toenails?

❖ ❖ ❖

"Why does my sweetheart always close her
eyes when I kiss her?"
    "Look in the mirror and you'll know."

John: You must marry me. I love you; there can
    be no one other . . .

Mary: But, John, I don't love you . . . you must find some other woman . . . some beautiful woman . . .

John: But I don't want a beautiful woman . . . I want you.

❖ ❖ ❖

Boy: You know, sweetheart, since I met you, I can't eat . . . I can't sleep . . . I can't drink.

Girl: Why not?

Boy: I'm broke.

❖ ❖ ❖

"My girlfriend takes advantage of me."

"What do you mean?"

"I invited her out to dinner, and she asked me if she could bring a date!"

❖ ❖ ❖

After a blind date a fellow mentioned to his friend: "After I got home last night, I felt a lump in my throat."

"You really like her, huh?"

"No, she's a karate expert."

❖ ❖ ❖

Girl: Will you marry me?

Boy: No, but I'll always admire your good taste.

"Do you have the book *Man, Master of Women*?" a young man asked the librarian.

"Fiction counter to your left," the librarian replied.

❖ ❖ ❖

Boy, with one hand cupped over the other: If you can guess what I have in my hand, I'll take you out tonight.
Girl: An elephant!
Boy: Nope! But that's close enough. I'll pick you up at 7:30.

❖ ❖ ❖

A schoolboy took home a library book whose cover read *How to Hug*, only to discover that it was volume seven of an encyclopedia!

❖ ❖ ❖

Boy: Ah, look at the cow and the calf rubbing noses in the pasture. That sight makes me want to do the same.
Girl: Well, go ahead . . . it's your cow.

❖ ❖ ❖

Girl: Do you think you could be happy with a girl like me?
Boy: Perhaps . . . if she isn't too much like you.

✧ ✧ ✧

"How come you go steady with Eloise?"
"She's different from other girls."
"How so?"
"She's the only girl who will go with me."

He: Oh, my dear, how can I leave you?
She: By train, plane, or taxi!

Boy: Gladys, do you love me?
Girl: Yeah.
Boy: Would you be willing to live on my
income?
Girl: Yes, if you'll get another for yourself.

✧ ✧ ✧

Girl: I'm telling you for the last time—you can't
kiss me!
Boy: I knew you would weaken!

✧ ✧ ✧

Girl: Do you love me?
Boy: Yes, dear.
Girl: Would you die for me?
Boy: No . . . mine is an undying love.

❖ ❖ ❖

John: Don't you think I'm rather good looking?
Judy: In a way.
John: What kind of way?
Judy: Away off.

❖ ❖ ❖

Bill: That girl in the red dress isn't very smart.
Phil: I know. She hasn't paid any attention to me either.

❖ ❖ ❖

She: Look at my engagement ring.
Chi-Chi: That's a lovely ring. It's nice to know you're not marrying a spendthrift.

❖ ❖ ❖

Boy: Boy, if I had a nickel for every girl I've kissed . . .
Girl: You'd be able to buy a pack of gum!

Cannibals

My uncle is a cannibal. He's been living on us for 20 years.

❖ ❖ ❖

First cannibal: We've just captured a movie star.
Second cannibal: Great! I was hoping for a good
    ham sandwich.

❖ ❖ ❖

Then there's the missionary the cannibal couldn't boil. He was a friar.

❖ ❖ ❖

Cannibal cook: Shall I stew both of these Navy
    cooks?
Cannibal king: No. One's enough. Too many
    cooks spoil the broth.

❖ ❖ ❖

A resourceful missionary fell into the hands of a band of cannibals.

"Going to eat me, I take it," said the missionary. "You wouldn't like me." He took out his pocketknife, sliced a piece from the calf of his leg, and handed it to the chief. "Try it and see for yourself," he urged.

The chief took one bite, grunted, and spat.

The missionary remained on the island 50 years. He had a cork leg.

9

Church, Preachers, and Sunday School

Reverend Henry Ward Beecher entered Plymouth Church one Sunday and found several letters awaiting him. He opened one and found it contained the single word, "Fool."

Quietly and with becoming seriousness he shared the letter with the congregation and announced: "I have known many an instance of a person writing a letter and forgetting to sign his name, but this is the only instance I have ever known of someone signing his name and forgetting to write the letter."

❖ ❖ ❖

Did you hear about the church janitor who also played the piano on Sunday? He watched his keys and pews.

❖ ❖ ❖

Did you hear about the country parson who decided to buy himself a horse? The dealer assured him that the one he selected was a perfect choice.

"This here horse," he said, "has lived all his life in a religious atmosphere. So remember that he'll never start if you order 'Giddy-up.' You've got to say, 'Praise the Lord.' Likewise, a 'Whoa' will never make him stop. You've got to say, 'Amen.' "

Thus forewarned, the parson paid for the horse, mounted him, and with a cheery "Praise the Lord" sent him cantering off in the direction of his parish. Suddenly he noticed that the road ahead had been washed out, leaving a chasm 200 yards deep.

In a panic, he forgot his instructions and cried "Whoa" in vain several times. The horse just cantered on. At the very last moment he remembered to cry "Amen" . . . and the horse stopped just short of the brink of the chasm. But alas! That's when the parson, out of force of habit, murmured fervently, "Praise the Lord!"

❖ ❖ ❖

A conscientious minister decided to get acquainted with a new family in his congregation and called on them one spring evening.

After his knock on the door, a lilting voice from within called out, "Is that you, Angel?"

"No," replied the minister, "but I'm from the same department."

❖ ❖ ❖

A young businessman returned home after a tough day at the office and found his two daughters, both about kindergarten age, acting up pretty boisterously. He scolded them and sent them off to bed. The next morning he found a note stuck on his bedroom door: "Be good to your children, and they will be good to you. God."

❖ ❖ ❖

Did you hear the one about the ministers who formed a bowling team? They called themselves the Holy Rollers.

❖ ❖ ❖

A preacher was called upon to substitute for the regular minister, who had failed to reach the church because he was delayed in a snowstorm. The speaker began by explaining the meaning of a substitute. "If you break a window," he said, "and then place cardboard there instead, that is a substitute."

After the sermon, a woman who had listened intently shook hands with him and, wishing to

compliment him, said, "You were no substitute
. . . you were a real pane!"

❖ ❖ ❖

The sermon went on and on and on in the
heat of the church. At last the minister paused
and asked, "What more, my friends, can I say?"

In the back of the church a voice offered
earnestly: "Amen!"

❖ ❖ ❖

Little Jane, whose grandmother was visiting
her family, was going to bed when her mother
called, "Don't forget to include Grandma in your
prayers tonight—that God should bless her and
let her live to be very, very old."

"Oh, she's old enough," replied Jane. "I'd
rather pray that God would make her young."

❖ ❖ ❖

A minister wound up the services one morning by saying, "Next Sunday I am going to
preach on the subject of liars. And in this con-
nection, as a preparation for my discourse, I
should like you all to read the seventeenth chapter of Mark."

On the following Sunday, the preacher rose
to begin and said, "Now, then, all of you who
have done as requested and read Mark 17,
please raise your hands."

Nearly every hand in the congregation went up.

Then said the preacher, "You are the people I want to talk to. There is no seventeenth chapter of Mark!"

❖ ❖ ❖

Why are there so few men with whiskers in heaven?

Because most men get in by a close shave.

❖ ❖ ❖

Little Susie, a six-year-old, complained, "Mother, I've got a stomachache."

"That's because your stomach is empty," the mother replied. "You would feel better if you had something in it."

That afternoon the minister visited and, in conversation, remarked he had been suffering all day with a severe headache.

Susie perked up. "That's because it's empty," she said. "You'd feel better if you had something in it."

❖ ❖ ❖

"Why do you keep reading your Bible all day long?" a youngster demanded of his grandfather.

"Well," he explained, "you might say I am cramming for my final examinations."

✧ ✧ ✧

A minister spoke to a deacon and said, "I'm told you went to the ball game instead of church this morning."

"That's a lie," said the deacon, "and here's the fish to prove it."

✧ ✧ ✧

A hat was passed around the church congregation for an offering for the visiting minister.

Presently it was returned to him . . . conspicuously and embarrassingly empty. Slowly and deliberately the parson inverted the hat and shook it meaningfully. Then raising his eyes to heaven, he exclaimed fervently, "I thank thee, dear Lord, that I got my hat back from this congregation."

✧ ✧ ✧

Hoping to develop his son's character, a father once gave him a penny and a quarter as he was leaving for Sunday school. "Now, Bill, you put whichever one you want in the offering plate," he said.

When the boy returned, his father asked which coin he had given. Bill answered, "Well, just before they sent around the plate the preacher said 'The Lord loveth a cheerful giver,' and I knew

I could give the penny a lot more cheerfully than I could give the quarter, so I gave it."

❖ ❖ ❖

A minister asked a little girl what she thought of her first church service.

"The music was nice," she said, "but the commercial was too long."

❖ ❖ ❖

A couple was touring the capitol in Washington D.C., and the guide pointed out a tall, benevolent gentleman as the congressional chaplain.

The lady asked, "What does the chaplain do? Does he pray for the Senate or House?"

The guide answered, "No, he gets up, looks at the Congress, then prays for the country!"

❖ ❖ ❖

Three sons of a lawyer, a doctor, and a minister were talking about how much money their fathers made.

The lawyer's son said, "My father goes into court on a case and often comes home with as much as $1500."

The doctor's son said, "My father performs an operation and earns as much as $2000."

The minister's son, determined not to be outdone, said, "That's nothing. My father preaches for just 20 minutes on Sunday morning and it takes four men to carry the money."

❖ ❖ ❖

The new preacher, at his first service, had a pitcher of water and a glass on the pulpit. As he preached, he drank until the pitcher of water was completely gone.

After the service someone asked an old woman of the church, "How did you like the new pastor?"

"Fine," she said, "but he's the first windmill I ever saw that was run by water."

❖ ❖ ❖

After a long, dry sermon, the minister announced that he wished to meet with the church board following the close of the service. The first man to arrive was a stranger. "You mis-understood my announcement. This is a meeting of the board," said the minister.

"I know," said the man, "but if there is any-one here more bored than I am, I'd like to meet him."

❖ ❖ ❖

There was a certain energetic young preacher who had a thriving country church. He was always prodding his people to do greater things for God, and he spent much time in preparation of his sermons.

There was a deacon in his congregation who did little and seemed to care less. It caused the young preacher much concern. On several occasions the preacher would tell him exactly what he thought. The old deacon never caught the point. The old deacon always thought he was referring to someone else. One Sunday, the preacher made it plainer as to whom he was talking. Following the service the deacon said, "Preacher, you sure told them today."

The next sermon was still more pointed than ever.

Again the deacon said, "Preacher, you sure told them today."

The next Sunday it rained so hard that no one was at the church except this one deacon. The preacher thought that he would now know about whom he was talking. The sermon went straight to the deacon who was the only one in the congregation. Following the service, the deacon walked up to the preacher and said, "Preacher, you sure told them if they had been here."

❖ ❖ ❖

A Sunday school teacher asked Little Willie who the first man in the Bible was.

"Hoss," said Willie.

"No," said the teacher. "It was Adam."

"Ah, shucks!" Willie replied. "I knew it was one of those Cartwrights."

❖ ❖ ❖

My son is such an introvert he can't even lead in silent prayer.

❖ ❖ ❖

A minister forgot the name of a couple he was going to marry so he said from the pulpit, "Will those wishing to be united in holy matrimony please come forward after the service."

After the service 13 old maids came forward.

❖ ❖ ❖

A new preacher had just begun his sermon. He was a little nervous and about ten minutes into the talk his mind went blank. He remembered what they had taught him in seminary when a situation like this would arise—repeat your last point. Often this would help you remember what is coming next. So he thought he would give it a try.

"Behold, I come quickly," he said. Still his mind was blank. He thought he would try it again. "Behold, I come quickly." Still nothing.

He tried it one more time with such force he fell forward, knocking the pulpit to one side, tripping over a flowerpot and falling into the lap of a little old lady in the front row.

The young preacher apologized and tried to explain what happened.

"That's all right, young man," said the lady. "It was my fault. I should have gotten out of the way. You told me three times you were coming!"

✧ ✧ ✧

Old Pete was very close to dying but made a miraculous recovery. In the hospital his pastor came to visit him.

"Tell me, Pete, when you were so near death's door, were you afraid to meet your Maker?"

"No, Pastor," said Pete. "It was the other man I was afraid of!"

✧ ✧ ✧

A Sunday school teacher asked her students to draw a picture of Jesus' family. After the pictures were brought to her, she saw that some of the youngsters had drawn the conventional pictures—the family and the manger, the family riding on the mule, and so on.

But she called up one little boy to ask him to explain his drawing, which showed an airplane with four heads sticking out of the windows.

She said, "I can understand you drew three of the heads to show Joseph, Mary, and Jesus. But who's the fourth head?"

"Oh," answered the boy, "that's Pontius the pilot!"

✧ ✧ ✧

Pastor: Isn't this a beautiful church? And here's a plaque for the men who died in the service.
Man: Which one . . . morning or evening?

✧ ✧ ✧

One friend to another: "You drive the car and I'll pray."
"What's the matter? Don't you trust my driving?"
"Don't you trust my praying?"

✧ ✧ ✧

Member: Pastor, how did you get that cut on your face?
Pastor: I was thinking about my sermon this morning and wasn't concentrating on what I was doing so I cut myself while shaving.
Member: That's too bad! Next time you'd better concentrate on your shaving and cut your sermon!

✧ ✧ ✧

A parishioner had dozed off during the morning service.
"Will all who want to go to heaven stand?" the preacher asked.
All stood except the sleeping parishioner.

After they sat down, the pastor continued: "Well, will all who want to go to the other place stand?"

Someone suddenly dropped a songbook and the sleeping man jumped to his feet and stood sheepishly facing the preacher. He mumbled confusedly, "Well, preacher, I don't know what we're voting for, but it looks like you and I are the only ones for it."

✧ ✧ ✧

Right in the middle of the service, just before the sermon, one of the congregation remembered she had forgotten to turn off the gas under the roast. Hurriedly she scribbled a note and passed it to the usher to give to her husband. Unfortunately, the usher misunderstood her intention and took it to the pulpit. Unfolding the note, the preacher read aloud, "Please go home and turn off the gas."

✧ ✧ ✧

A little boy forgot his lines in a Sunday school presentation. His mother, sitting in the front row to prompt him, gestured and formed the words silently with her lips, but it didn't help. Her son's memory was blank.

Finally she leaned forward and whispered the cue, "I am the light of the world."

The child beamed and with great feeling and a loud, clear voice said, "My mother is the light of the world."

✧ ✧ ✧

Clara: My pastor is so good he can talk on any subject for an hour.

Sarah: That's nothing! My pastor can talk for an hour without a subject!

✧ ✧ ✧

Preacher: Please take it easy on the bill for repairing my car. Remember, I am a poor preacher.

Mechanic: I know; I heard you Sunday!

✧ ✧ ✧

Two men were bosom buddies. Much to the amazement of one, the other became a Sunday school teacher.

"I bet you don't even know the Lord's Prayer," the other man fumed.

"Everybody knows that," the other replied. "It's 'Now I lay me down to sleep. . .'"

"You win," said the other admiringly. "I didn't know you knew so much about the Bible."

✧ ✧ ✧

Member: How are you feeling, pastor?

Pastor: Better.

Member: We had a committee meeting the other night, and they voted to send you this get-well card. The motion passed 4 to 3!

❖ ❖ ❖

A Sunday school teacher asked a little girl if she said her prayers every night.

"No, not every night," declared the child. "'Cause some nights I don't want anything!"

❖ ❖ ❖

The chaplain was passing through the prison garment factory. "Sewing?" he asked a prisoner who was at work.

"No, chaplain," replied the prisoner gloomily, "reaping!"

❖ ❖ ❖

Correcting Sunday school lessons one day, a teacher found that little Jimmy had written: "Harold be Thy name" as well as "Give us this day our jelly bread."

❖ ❖ ❖

A Sunday school teacher asked her class to draw a picture illustrating a Bible story. One paper handed in contained a picture of a big car. An old man with long whiskers flying in the breeze was driving. A man and a woman were seated in the backseat. Puzzled, the teacher asked little Jimmy to explain his drawing. "Why, that is God. He's driving Adam and Eve out of the Garden of Eden."

❖ ❖ ❖

A hungry little boy was beginning to eat his dinner when his father reminded him that they hadn't prayed.

"We don't have to," said the little boy. "Mommy is a good cook!"

❖ ❖ ❖

Little Mary, the daughter of a radio announcer, was invited to a friend's house for dinner. The hostess asked if Mary would honor them by saying grace.

Delighted, the little girl cleared her throat, looked at her wristwatch, and said, "This good food, friends, is coming to you through the courtesy of Almighty God!"

❖ ❖ ❖

On the way home from church a little boy asked his mother, "Is it true, Mommy, that we are made of dust?"

"Yes, darling."

"And do we go back to dust again when we die?"

"Yes, dear."

"Well, Mommy, when I said my prayers last night and looked under the bed, I found someone who is either coming or going."

❖ ❖ ❖

One Sunday a farmer went to church. When he entered he saw that he and the preacher were the only ones present. The preacher asked the farmer if he wanted him to go ahead and preach. The farmer said, "I'm not too smart, but if I went to feed my cattle and only one showed up, I'd feed him." So the minister began his sermon.

One hour passed, then two hours, then two-and-a-half hours. The preacher finally finished and came down to ask the farmer how he had liked the sermon.

The farmer answered slowly, "Well, I'm not very smart, but if I went to feed my cattle and only one showed up, I sure wouldn't feed him all the hay."

❖ ❖ ❖

Little Susie concluded her prayer by saying: "Dear God, before I finish, please take care of Daddy, take care of Mommy, take care of my baby brother, Grandma, and Grandpa . . . and please, God, take care of yourself—or else we're all sunk!"

❖ ❖ ❖

A Sunday school teacher asked her class to write a composition on the story of Samson. One teenage girl wrote, "Samson wasn't so unusual. The boys I know brag about their strength and wear their hair long too."

❖ ❖ ❖

The teacher handed out the test papers and told the children they could start answering the questions.

She noticed little Billy sitting with his head bowed, his hands over his face. She approached him.

"Don't you feel well?" she inquired.

"Oh, I'm fine, teacher. I always pray before a test!"

❖ ❖ ❖

A minister was about to baptize a baby. Turning to the father, he inquired, "His name, please?"

"William Patrick Arthur Timothy John MacArthur."

The minister turned to his assistant and said, "A little more water, please."

❖ ❖ ❖

A little boy excited about his part in the Christmas play came home and said, "I got a part in the Christmas play!"

"What part?" asked his mother.

"I'm one of the three wise guys!" was the reply.

❖ ❖ ❖

St. Peter looked at the new arrival skeptically; he'd had no advance knowledge of his coming.

"How did you get here?" he asked.

"Flu."

❖ ❖ ❖

The boys were trying to outdo each other. The first said, "My uncle's a doctor. I can be sick for nothing!" The second youngster shot back, "Big deal! My uncle is a preacher. I can be good for nothing!"

❖ ❖ ❖

"Mommy," asked little Judy, "did you ever see a cross-eyed bear?"

"Why, no, Judy," chuckled her mother. "Why do you ask?"

"Well, in Sunday school this morning, we sang about 'the consecrated cross-eyed bear.' "

❖ ❖ ❖

The sermon was very long this Sunday morning and Donny was getting more restless by the minute.

Suddenly, in a whisper too loud for his mother's comfort, he blurted out, "If we give him the money now, Ma, will he let us go?"

❖ ❖ ❖

"Daddy, I want to ask you a question," said Bobby after his first day in Sunday school.

"Yes, Bobby, what is it?"

"The teacher was reading the Bible to us—all about the children of Israel building the temple, the children of Israel crossing the Red Sea, the children of Israel making sacrifices. Didn't the grown-ups do anything?"

❖ ❖ ❖

The young girl of the house, by way of punishment for some minor misdemeanor, was compelled to eat her dinner alone at a little table in a corner of the dining room. The rest of the family paid no attention to her presence until they heard her audibly praying over her repast: "I thank thee, Lord, for preparing a table before me in the presence of mine enemies."

❖ ❖ ❖

People who cough incessantly never seem to go to a doctor—they go to banquets, concerts, and church.

❖ ❖ ❖

Did you hear about the man from the income tax bureau who phoned a certain minister and said, "We're checking the tax return of a member of your church, and we noticed he listed a donation to your building fund of $300. Is that correct?"

The minister answered without hesitation, "I haven't got my records available, but I'll promise you one thing: If he hasn't he will!"

❖ ❖ ❖

The minister's daughter was sent to bed with a stomachache and missed her usual romp with her daddy. A few minutes later she appeared at the top of the stairs and called to her mother, "Mama, let me talk with Daddy."

"No, my dear, not tonight. Get back in bed."

"Please, Mama."

"I said 'no.' That's enough now."

"Mother, I'm a very sick woman, and I must see my pastor at once."

10

Crusty Characters

His trouble is too much bone in the head and not enough in the back.

✧ ✧ ✧

He has a concrete mind . . . permanently set and all mixed up.

✧ ✧ ✧

He's a man of rare intelligence . . . it's rare when he shows any.

✧ ✧ ✧

You know, if brains were dynamite, she wouldn't have enough to blow her nose!

❖ ❖ ❖

He's just as smart as he can be . . . unfortunately.

❖ ❖ ❖

She has a keen sense of rumor.

❖ ❖ ❖

You could make a fortune if you could buy him for what you think of him and sell him for what he thinks of himself.

❖ ❖ ❖

He's a second-story man; no one ever believes his first story.

❖ ❖ ❖

When she meets another egotist, it's an I for an I.

❖ ❖ ❖

He's always down on everything he's not up on.

❖ ❖ ❖

He doesn't want anyone to make a fuss over him . . . just to treat him as they would any other great man.

❖ ❖ ❖

Be careful when you're speaking about him . . . you're speaking of the man he loves.

❖ ❖ ❖

Someone should push the "down" button on her elevator shoes.

❖ ❖ ❖

She says that whenever she's down in the dumps she gets a new hat. I've always thought that's where she gets them.

❖ ❖ ❖

He has a great labor-saving device . . . tomorrow.

❖ ❖ ❖

He's a regular "Rock of Jello."

❖ ❖ ❖

She is so nervous that she keeps coffee awake.

❖ ❖ ❖

He's the real decisive type . . . he'll give you a definite "maybe."

❖ ❖ ❖

They call her "Jigsaw." Every time she's faced with a problem she goes to pieces.

❖ ❖ ❖

He left his job because of illness and fatigue. His boss got sick and tired of him.

❖ ❖ ❖

The only thing she's ever achieved on her own is dandruff.

❖ ❖ ❖

Some cause happiness wherever they go; others whenever they go.

❖ ❖ ❖

He had to see the doctor in the morning for a blood test, so he stayed up all night studying for it.

❖ ❖ ❖

She has delusions of glamour!

❖ ❖ ❖

He's one person who would make a perfect stranger!

✧ ✧ ✧

She made him a millionaire. Before she married him, he was a billionaire.

✧ ✧ ✧

He can stay longer in an hour than most people do in a week.

✧ ✧ ✧

When it comes to telling her age, she's shy . . . about ten years shy.

✧ ✧ ✧

There's no doubt he's trying. In fact, he's very trying.

✧ ✧ ✧

He stopped drinking coffee in the morning because it keeps him awake the rest of the day.

Do You Know?

How do you milk an ant?
First, you get a low stool . . .

❖ ❖ ❖

What's more clever than speaking in several
languages?
Keeping your mouth shut in one.

❖ ❖ ❖

How do you tune "hard rock" instruments?
You don't.

❖ ❖ ❖

What kind of fish do you eat with peanut
butter?
Jellyfish.

❖ ❖ ❖

When rain falls, does it ever get up again?
Yes, in dew time.

❖ ❖ ❖

What do you get when you cross a porcupine
   with a sheep?
An animal that knits its own sweaters.

❖ ❖ ❖

What happens when two bullets get married?
They have a little BB.

❖ ❖ ❖

What does the government use when it takes a
   census of all the monkeys in Africa?
An ape recorder.

❖ ❖ ❖

What do you get if you cross a chicken with an
   elephant?
*I don't know, but Colonel Sanders would have a lot of
   trouble trying to dip it into the batter.*

❖ ❖ ❖

If a dog lost his tail, where would he get another
   one?
At the retail store, naturally.

❖ ❖ ❖

Why does the ocean roar?
You would too if you had lobsters in your bed.

❖ ❖ ❖

What has four legs and flies?
A picnic table.

❖ ❖ ❖

What is the definition of a financial genius?
A person who can earn money faster than the family can spend it.

❖ ❖ ❖

What is another name for toupee?
Top secret.

❖ ❖ ❖

Why did Humpty Dumpty have a great fall?
To make up for a terrible summer.

❖ ❖ ❖

What's worse than a giraffe with a sore throat?
A hippopotamus with chapped lips.

❖ ❖ ❖

What do they call a man who still has his tonsils and appendix?
A doctor.

❖ ❖ ❖

How do you get rid of company that stays
too long?
Treat them like family.

❖ ❖ ❖

What is the longest word in the English
language?
*Smiles—because there's a mile between the first
and last letter.*

❖ ❖ ❖

What is the best way to keep fish from smelling?
Cut off their noses.

❖ ❖ ❖

What is more blessed to give than receive?
Advice.

❖ ❖ ❖

What do you call a person who crosses the ocean
twice without taking a bath?
A dirty double crosser.

❖ ❖ ❖

What animal has the smallest appetite?
A moth. It just eat holes.

❖ ❖ ❖

What book contains more stirring pages than
any other book?
A cookbook.

❖ ❖ ❖

Why should you always take a watch with you
when you cross the desert?
Because there is a spring in it.

❖ ❖ ❖

What is black and white and red all over?
A zebra with a sunburn.

❖ ❖ ❖

What do you call a camel without a hump?
Humphrey.

❖ ❖ ❖

What two words have the most letters?
Post office.

❖ ❖ ❖

If a man smashed a clock, could he be convicted
of killing time?
Not if he could prove that the clock struck first.

❖ ❖ ❖

What did the leftovers say when they were put
    into the freezer?
Foiled again.

❖ ❖ ❖

Where do jellyfish get their jelly?
From ocean currents.

❖ ❖ ❖

Is it difficult to eat soup with a mustache?
Yes, it is quite a strain.

❖ ❖ ❖

What is another name for a nursery?
Bawlroom.

❖ ❖ ❖

What do you call a monkey that sells potato
    chips?
A chipmonk.

❖ ❖ ❖

In what month do people talk the least?
February.

❖ ❖ ❖

What do you get when you cross an elephant
with a computer?
A 5,000-pound know-it-all.

❖ ❖ ❖

Why do people laugh up their sleeves?
Because that's where their funny bones are.

❖ ❖ ❖

What is the name of a tourniquet worn on the
left hand to stop circulation?
An engagement ring.

❖ ❖ ❖

How can you jump off a 50-foot ladder and not
get hurt?
Jump off the first rung.

❖ ❖ ❖

What machine scares the daylights into you?
An alarm clock.

❖ ❖ ❖

What's the difference between a mental institution and a college?
*In the mental institution you must show improve-
ment to get out.*

❖ ❖ ❖

If you have seven apples and I ask you for two,
how many would you have left?
Seven.

❖ ❖ ❖

What is another name for a juvenile delinquent?
Child hood.

❖ ❖ ❖

What is the difference between unlawful and
illegal?
An illegal is a sick bird.

❖ ❖ ❖

If all the people in the United States owned pink
cars, what would the country be called?
A pink carnation.

Education

A wise schoolteacher sends this note to all parents on the first day of school: "If you promise not to believe everything your child says happens at school, I'll promise not to believe everything he or she says happens at home."

❖ ❖ ❖

Teacher: What are you—animal, vegetable, or mineral?
Little boy: Vegetable. I'm a human bean!

❖ ❖ ❖

Tony: My college has turned out some great men.
Daisy: I didn't know you were a college graduate.
Tony: I'm one they turned out!

❖ ❖ ❖

It was the little girl's first day at school, and the teacher was making out her registration card.

"What is your father's name?" she asked.

"Daddy," replied the child.

"Yes, I know, but what does your mother call him?"

"Oh, she doesn't call him anything. She likes him!"

❖ ❖ ❖

Teacher: Why don't you brush your teeth? I can see what you had for breakfast this morning.
Student: What did I have?
Teacher: Eggs!
Student: You're wrong! That was yesterday!

❖ ❖ ❖

Girl: Too bad you flunked the test. How far were you from the right answer?
Boy: Two seats!

❖ ❖ ❖

A young college student had stayed up all night studying for his zoology test the next day. As he entered the classroom, he saw ten stands with ten birds on them. Each bird had a sack over its head; only the legs were showing. He sat right in the front row because he wanted to do the best job possible. The professor announced that the test would be to look at each of the birds' legs and give the common name, habitat, genus, and species.

The student looked at each of the birds' legs. They all looked the same to him. He began to get upset. He had stayed up all night studying and now had to identify birds by their legs. The more he thought about it the madder he got.

Finally he could stand it no longer. He went up to the professor's desk and said, "What a stupid test! How could anyone tell the difference between birds by looking at their legs?" With that the student threw his test on the professor's desk and walked to the door.

The professor was surprised. The class was so big that he didn't know every student's name so as the student reached the door the professor called, "Mister, what's your name?"

The enraged student pulled up his pant legs and said, "You tell me, buddy! You tell me!"

❖ ❖ ❖

A father was examining his son's report card. "One thing is definitely in your favor," he announced. "With this report card, you couldn't possibly be cheating."

❖ ❖ ❖

There's one great thing to be said for a college education. It enables you to worry about things all over the world.

A college student with coin in hand said: "If it's heads, I go to bed. If it's tails, I stay up. If it stands on edge, I study."

Professor: If there are any dumbbells in the room, please stand up.

There was a long pause, then a lone freshman stood up in the rear.

Professor: What? Do you consider yourself a dumbbell?

Freshman: Well, not exactly, but I hate to see you standing all alone.

Teacher: Johnny, give me a sentence with a direct object.

Johnny: Teacher, everybody thinks you're beautiful.

Teacher: Thank you, Johnny, but what is the object?

Johnny: A good report card.

Teacher: If your mother gave you a large apple
and a small one, then told you to share with
your brother, which one would you give him?
Johnnie: Do you mean my little brother or my
big brother?

❖ ❖ ❖

For weeks a six-year-old lad kept telling his
first-grade teacher about the baby brother or sister that was expected at his house. Then one day
the mother allowed the boy to feel the move-
ments of the unborn child. The six-year-old was
obviously impressed, but made no comment.
Furthermore, he stopped telling his teacher
about the impending event.

The teacher finally sat down with the boy
and said, "Tommy, whatever has become of that
baby brother or sister you were expecting at
home?"

Tommy burst into tears and confessed, "I
think Mommy ate it!"

❖ ❖ ❖

Librarian: Please be quiet. The people next to
you can't read.
Girl: What a shame! I've been reading since I
was six.

❖ ❖ ❖

Teacher: Billy, what did you do when Ed called you a liar?

Billy: I remembered what you told me: "A soft answer turns away anger."

Teacher: Very good, Billy. What answer did you give him?

Billy: I answered him with a soft tomato.

❖ ❖ ❖

Teacher: Really, Tommy, your handwriting is terrible! You must learn to write better.

Tommy: Well, if I did, you'd be finding fault with my spelling.

❖ ❖ ❖

Teacher: What is an emperor?

Georgia: I don't know.

Teacher: An emperor is a ruler.

Georgia: Oh, sure. I used to carry an emperor to school with me.

❖ ❖ ❖

"Some plants," said the teacher, "have the prefix 'dog.' For instance, there is the dogrose, the dogwood, and the dogviolet. Who can name another plant prefixed by 'dog'?"

"I can," shouted a little boy in the back row. "Collieflower."

❖ ❖ ❖

As a special treat, a teacher took her class to visit a museum of natural history. The children returned home excitedly. On rushing into his house, one of the little boys greeted his mother exuberantly: "What do you think we did today, Mother? The teacher took us to a dead circus!"

❖ ❖ ❖

Interrupted by the sound of the bell announcing the end of the class, the professor was annoyed to see the students noisily preparing to leave although he was in the middle of his lecture. "Just a moment, gentlemen," he said, "I have a few more pearls to cast."

❖ ❖ ❖

Teacher: Johnny, how much is three times three.
Johnny: Nine.
Teacher: That's pretty good.
Johnny: Pretty good? Say, "It's perfect.'"

❖ ❖ ❖

He was in school so long the other pupils used to bring him apples thinking he was the teacher.

❖ ❖ ❖

Sometimes you wonder what kids are really learning. Yesterday a teacher pointed at the flag, turned to my six-year-old, and asked him what it was.

He answered, "It is the flag of my country!"

The teacher couldn't leave well enough alone. She said, "Now tell me the name of the country."

And he said, " 'Tis of thee!' "

❖ ❖ ❖

Teacher: I hope I didn't see you looking at some-one else's paper, Billy.

Billy: I hope so, too, Teacher.

❖ ❖ ❖

Student: I don't think I deserve a zero on this test!

Teacher: Neither do I, but it's the lowest mark I can give you.

❖ ❖ ❖

A college boy to his mother: "I decided that I want to be a political science major, and I want to clean up the mess in the world!"

"That's very nice," purred his mother. "You can go upstairs and start with your room."

❖ ❖ ❖

A student wrote the following on his preChristmas examination paper: "God only knows the answer to this question. Merry Christmas!"

The professor returned the paper with the following notation: "God gets an 'A'; you get an 'F.' Happy New Year."

✧ ✧ ✧

Teacher: Where's your homework this morning?
Student: You'll never believe this, but on the way to school I made a paper airplane out of it and someone hijacked it to Cuba!

✧ ✧ ✧

Teacher: What do you call a person who keeps on talking when people are no longer interested?
Student: A teacher.

✧ ✧ ✧

Teacher: What's the formula for water?
Student: H,I,J,K,L,M,N,O.
Teacher: That's not the formula I gave you.
Student: Yes, it is. You said it was H to O.

⟨13⟩

Family Frolic

Girl: The man I marry must stand out in company, be musical, tell jokes, line dance, and stay at home nights.
Mother: You don't want a husband—you want a TV set.

❖ ❖ ❖

Father pacing the floor with a wailing baby in his arms as his wife lies snug in bed: "No one ever asks me how I manage to combine marriage and a career."

❖ ❖ ❖

My children are at the perfect age . . . too old to cry at night and too young to borrow my car.

❖ ❖ ❖

When the father called home, the six-year-old son answered and said, "Don't talk too loud, Dad, the babysitter is asleep."

❖ ❖ ❖

Friend: How is your new "doctor" son getting along in his practice?

Mother: Fine. He is doing so well he can occasionally tell a patient there is nothing the matter with him.

❖ ❖ ❖

Father: Why don't you get a job?

Son: Why?

Father: So you can earn some money.

Son: Why?

Father: So you can put some money in a bank account and earn interest.

Son: Why?

Father: So that when you're old you can use the money in your bank account and never have to work again.

Son: But, I'm not working now!

❖ ❖ ❖

Son: Here's my report card, Dad, along with one of your old ones I found in the attic.

Father: Well, son, you're right. This old report
    card of mine you found isn't any better than
    yours. I guess the only fair thing to do is give
    you what my father gave me.

❖ ❖ ❖

Son: Dad, what is "creeping inflation"?
Father: It's when your mother starts out asking
    for new shoes and ends up with a complete
    new outfit.

❖ ❖ ❖

The best way for a stay-at-home mom to get
a few minutes to herself at the end of the day is
to start doing the dishes.

❖ ❖ ❖

Father: Do you think it will improve Junior's
    behavior if we buy him a bicycle?
Mother: No, but it'll spread it over a wider area.

❖ ❖ ❖

Mother to fussy son: Twenty years from now
    you'll be telling some girl what a great cook
    your mother was . . . now eat your dinner.

❖ ❖ ❖

Father to teenage son: Do you mind if I use the
    car tonight? I'm taking your mother out and I
    want to impress her.

❖ ❖ ❖

Mother: Every time you're naughty I get another gray hair.

Son: Gee, Mom, you must have been a terror when you were young . . . just look at Grandma.

❖ ❖ ❖

Son: Dad, will you help me find the least common denominator in this math problem?

Dad: Don't tell me that hasn't been found—they were looking for it when I was a kid.

Photographer (to young man): It will make a much better picture if you put your hand on your father's shoulder.

Father: It would be much more natural if he had his hand in my pocket.

❖ ❖ ❖

Two cub scouts whose younger brother had fallen into a shallow pond rushed home to Mother with tears in their eyes. "We're trying to give him artificial respiration," one of them sobbed, "but he keeps getting up and walking away."

❖ ❖ ❖

Mother: Donna, you shouldn't always keep
everything for yourself. I've told you before
that you should let your little brother play
with your toys half of the time.
Donna: I've been doing that. I take the sled
going downhill, and he takes it going up.

❖ ❖ ❖

In a country home that seldom had guests,
the young son was eager to help his mother after
his father appeared with two dinner guests from
the office.

When the dinner was nearly over, the boy
went to the kitchen and proudly carried in the
first piece of apple pie, giving it to his father,
who passed it to a guest.

The boy came in with a second piece of pie
and gave it to his father, who again gave it to a
guest.

This was too much for the boy, who said,
"It's no use, Dad. The pieces are all the same
size."

❖ ❖ ❖

Little Billy was left to fix lunch. When his
mother returned with a friend, she noticed that
Billy had already strained the tea.

"Did you find the tea strainer?" his mother
asked.

"No, mother, I couldn't, so I used the fly swatter," replied Billy.

His mother nearly fainted, so Billy hastily added, "Don't get excited, Mother. I used an old one."

✧ ✧ ✧

The 12-year-old boy stood patiently beside the clock counter while the store clerk waited on all of the adult customers. Finally he got around to the youngster, who made his purchase and hurried out to the curb, where his father was impatiently waiting in his car.

"What took you so long, son?" he asked.

"The man waited on everybody in the store before me," the boy replied. "But I got even."

"How?"

"I wound and set all the alarm clocks while I was waiting," the youngster explained happily. "It's going to be a mighty noisy place at eight o'clock."

✧ ✧ ✧

Mother: Were you a good boy in school today?
Son: How much trouble can you get into standing in a corner all day?

❖ ❖ ❖

"Did you see how pleased Mrs. Smith looked when I told her she didn't look a day older than her daughter?"

"I didn't notice Mrs. Smith. . . . I was too busy watching the expression on the daughter's face!"

❖ ❖ ❖

First man: I keep a gun handy in case anyone breaks into my house.

Second man: If a burglar came into our bedroom during the night, I'd get up and take him to the bathroom.

❖ ❖ ❖

"Young man," said the angry father from the head of the stairs, "didn't I hear the clock strike four when you brought my daughter in?"

"You did," admitted the boyfriend. "It was going to strike eleven, but I grabbed it and held the gong so it wouldn't disturb you."

The father muttered, "Doggone! Why didn't I think of that one in my courting days!"

14

Famous Last Words

"You can make it easy . . . that train isn't coming fast."

✧ ✧ ✧

"Gimme a match. I think my gas tank is empty."

✧ ✧ ✧

"Wife, these biscuits are tough."

✧ ✧ ✧

"Step on her, boy, we're only going 75."

✧ ✧ ✧

"Just watch me dive from that bridge."

✧ ✧ ✧

"If you knew anything you wouldn't be a traffic cop."

"What? Your mother is going to stay another month?"

"Say, who's boss of this joint, anyhow?"

Food

A man walked into a restaurant in a strange town. The waiter came and asked him for his order. Feeling lonely, he replied, "Meat loaf and a kind word." When the waiter returned with the meat loaf, the man said, "Where's the good word?"

The waiter put down the meat loaf and sighed, bent down, and whispered, "Don't eat the meat loaf."

✧ ✧ ✧

Cook: Do you want me to cut this pizza into six or eight pieces?
Man: You'd better make it six. . . . I don't think I can eat eight pieces!

Customer: Do you serve crabs in this dump?
Waiter: Yes, sir. What'll you have?

❖ ❖ ❖

"Waiter!" shouted an irate customer. "I can't tell whether this is coffee or tea! It tastes like gasoline!"

"If it tastes like gasoline then it positively is coffee," the waiter said. "Our tea tastes like turpentine."

❖ ❖ ❖

"Waiter," said the surprised customer as he examined his check, "What's this eight dollars for?"

"For the chopped liver sandwich, sir."

"Yeah?" The customer nodded. "Whose liver was it—the president's?"

❖ ❖ ❖

The manager of a restaurant called his waitresses together. "Women," he began, "I want you to all look your best today. Greet every customer with a smile and a kind word."

"What's up?" asked one of the women. "Bunch of big shots coming in today?"

"No, the meat's tough today."

Customer: Those franks you sold me were meat at one end and cornmeal at the other!
Butcher: Yes, ma'am. In these times it's difficult to make both ends meat.

❖ ❖ ❖

Man: I can't eat this food! Call the manager!
Waitress: It's no use, sir. He can't eat it either.

❖ ❖ ❖

A meek little man in a restaurant timidly touched the arm of a man putting on an overcoat. "Excuse me," he said, "but do you happen to be Mr. Smith of Newport?"

"No, I'm not!" the man answered impatiently.

"Oh—er—well," stammered the first man, "you see, I am, and that's his overcoat you're putting on."

❖ ❖ ❖

Sign in a restaurant: Our customers are always right: misinformed, perhaps, inexact, bullheaded, fickle, even downright stupid, but never wrong.

❖ ❖ ❖

Joe: A panhandler came up to me and said he
hadn't had a bite in two weeks.
Moe: Poor fellow. What did you do?
Joe: Bit him of course!

❖ ❖ ❖

I know a woman who has cooked so many
TV dinners she thinks she's in show business.

❖ ❖ ❖

Man: Do you serve breakfast here?
Waitress: Sure; what'll it be?
Man: Let me have watery scrambled eggs . . .
some burnt toast . . . and some weak coffee,
lukewarm.
Waitress: Whatever you say, sir.
Man: Now, are you doing anything while that
order is going through?
Waitress: Why—no, sir.
Man: Then sit here and nag me awhile. . . . I'm
homesick!

I hate to always eat and run, but the way I
tip it's the only safe procedure.

❖ ❖ ❖

Customer: Your sign says, "$50 to anyone who orders something we can't furnish." I would like to have an elephant ear sandwich.
Waiter: Ohhh . . . we're going to have to pay you the $50.
Customer: No elephant ears, huh?
Waiter: Oh, we've got lots of them . . . but we're all out of those big buns!

❖ ❖ ❖

"A fellow walked up to me today and asked for a dollar for a cup of coffee. I gave it to him, and then followed him clear across town to the restaurant."

❖ ❖ ❖

Customer: What flavors of ice cream do you have?
Hoarse waiter: Vanilla, strawberry, and choco-late.
Customer: Do you have laryngitis?
Waiter: No, just vanilla, strawberry, and choco-late.

❖ ❖ ❖

Shopper: The way food prices are going up, it soon will be cheaper to eat the money.

❖ ❖ ❖

Diner: What would you recommend for tonight?
Waiter: Go someplace else . . . the cook is on
   strike.

❖ ❖ ❖

Percy: I won't criticize their chef, but you'll
   notice three shakers on every table . . . salt,
   pepper, and Alka-Seltzer.

❖ ❖ ❖

Waiter: Would you like your coffee black?
Customer: What other colors do you have?

❖ ❖ ❖

Diner: What's this fly doing in my soup?
Waiter: The backstroke.

❖ ❖ ❖

Customer: Waitress, why is my doughnut all
   smashed?
Waitress: You said you wanted a cup of coffee
   and a doughnut, and step on it.

❖ ❖ ❖

Waiter: And how did you find your steak, sir?
Customer: I just lifted one of the brussels
   sprouts and there it was!

✧ ✧ ✧

Customer: This food isn't fit for a pig!
Waiter: I'm sorry, sir. I'll bring you some that is.

✧ ✧ ✧

Tim: Look, Jim, why are you always trying to
impress me? So you spoke to the waiter in
French! So, big deal! So what good is it to
know French? . . .What did he tell you,
waiter?
Waiter: He told me to give you the check, sir!

Customer: Your sign says, "Any sandwich you
can name." I would like a whale sandwich.
Waiter: Okay. (He disappears into the kitchen
and shortly returns.) I'm afraid I can't get you
a whale sandwich.
Customer: Why not? . . .your sign says "any
sandwich."
Waiter: The cook says he doesn't want to start a
new whale for one lousy sandwich.

◇16◇

Getting Older

Middle age is when you know all the answers and nobody asks you the questions.

❖ ❖ ❖

Three states of man: youth, middle age, "you're looking fine!"

❖ ❖ ❖

There are three ways to tell if you are getting old: first, a loss of memory; second . . .

❖ ❖ ❖

The hardest decision in life is when to start middle age.

❖ ❖ ❖

Middle age is when the narrow waist and the broad mind begin to change places.

Golf

Bill: I'd move heaven and earth to break my 100 score.
Phil: Try moving heaven. You've already moved plenty of earth today.

Caddy: Let me say this about your game, mister. I wouldn't say you were the worst golfer I have seen on this course, but I've seen places today that I've never seen before.

"Look," the golfer screamed at his caddy, "if you don't keep your big mouth shut, you'll drive me out of my mind."

"That's no drive, mister," corrected the caddy. "That's a putt."

❖ ❖ ❖

Golfer: Notice any improvement since last year?
Caddy: Polished your clubs, didn't you?

❖ ❖ ❖

Golfer: Why do you keep looking at your watch?
Caddy: This isn't a watch, sir. It's a compass.

❖ ❖ ❖

Golfer: The doctor says I can't play golf.
Caddy: Oh, he's played with you, too, huh?

❖ ❖ ❖

"Caddy, why didn't you see where that ball went?"

"Well, it doesn't usually go anywhere, Mrs. Smith. You caught me off-guard."

❖ ❖ ❖

The other day I was playing golf and saw an unusual thing. A golfer became so mad that he threw his brand-new set of golf clubs into the lake. A few minutes later he came back, waded into the lake, and retrieved his clubs. He proceeded to take his car keys out of the bag—then threw the clubs back into the water.

❖ ❖ ❖

Golfer: Well, what do you think of my game?
Caddy: I guess it's all right, but I still like golf
better.

✧ ✧ ✧

Golfer: How would you have played that last
shot, caddy?
Caddy: Under an assumed name!

✧ ✧ ✧

Golfer: You must be the world's worst caddy!
Caddy: No, sir! That would be too much of a
coincidence!

Hot Air

A speaker was having a little trouble getting started in his speech. All of the sudden someone from the audience shouted: "Tell 'em all you know. It will only take a minute."

"I'll tell 'em all we both know," shot back the speaker. "It won't take any longer."

✧ ✧ ✧

A manufacturer of bicycle tires was the speaker at a business luncheon. In response to a toast, he said: "I have no desire or intention to inflict upon you a long speech for it is well known in our trade that the longer the spoke, the bigger the tire."

✧ ✧ ✧

Once during a debate Abraham Lincoln was accused by Stephen Douglas of being two-faced.

Without hesitation Lincoln calmly replied, "I leave it to my audience . . . if I had two faces, would I be wearing this one?"

✧ ✧ ✧

"That was a great speech, sir. I like the straightforward way you dodged those issues."

✧ ✧ ✧

At a lecture series a very poor speaker was on the platform. As he was speaking, people in the audience began to get up and leave. After about ten minutes there was only one man left. Finally the man stopped speaking and asked the man why he remained to the end.

"I'm the next speaker," was the reply.

✧ ✧ ✧

A lecturer announced to his audience that the world would probably end in seven billion years.

"How long did you say?" came a terrified voice from the rear.

"Seven billion years."

"Thank goodness!" said the voice. "I thought for a moment you said seven million."

19

It's All in the Family

Advice to mothers: Unless you deliberately set aside a little time for regular relaxation, you will not be able to efficiently care for your family. Therefore, plan to relax a minimum of an hour-and-a-half every 15 years.

❖ ❖ ❖

One day Johnny's father brought his boss home for dinner. When Johnny's mother served the meat, the little boy asked, "Is this mutton?"

The mother replied, "No. Why do you ask?"

"Because Dad said he was going to bring home a muttonhead for dinner," Johnny answered.

❖ ❖ ❖

Adolescence is a period of rapid changes. Between the ages of 12 and 17, for example, a child may see his parents age 20 years.

❖ ❖ ❖

After dinner, members of a lot of families suffer from dishtemper.

❖ ❖ ❖

Father: What's wrong, Judy? Usually you talk on the phone for hours. This time you only talked half an hour. How come?
Judy: It was a wrong number.

❖ ❖ ❖

A father, whose looks aren't anything to brag about, tells this on himself:

My little girl was sitting on my lap facing a mirror. After gazing intently at her reflection for some minutes, she said, "Daddy, did God make you?"

"Certainly, my dear," I told her.

"And did He make me, too?" she asked, taking another look in the mirror.

"Certainly, dear. What makes you ask?"

"Seems to me He's doing better work lately."

❖ ❖ ❖

A letter from a college student said, "Please send food packages! All they serve here is breakfast, lunch, and dinner."

❖ ❖ ❖

Mother: Aunt Mathilda won't kiss you with that
    dirty face.
Boy: That's what I figured.

❖ ❖ ❖

"Dear Dad: Let me hear from you more
often, even if it's only a five or ten."

❖ ❖ ❖

"In our family," a little girl told her teacher,
"everybody marries relatives. My father married
my mother, my uncle married my aunt, and the
other day I found out that my grandmother married my grandfather."

❖ ❖ ❖

Father: Well, son, what did you learn in school
    today?
Son: I learned to say, "Yes, sir," and "No, sir,"
    and "Yes, ma'am," and "No, ma'am."
Father: Really?
Son: Yeah!

❖ ❖ ❖

Nowadays you'll find almost everything in
the average American home . . . except the family.

❖ ❖ ❖

Father of teenage son to neighbor: Junior's at
that awkward age . . . too old for a spanking
and too young for analysis.

❖ ❖ ❖

Son: Dad, the Bible says if you don't let me have
the car, you hate me.
Father: Where does it say that?
Son: Proverbs 13:24—"He that spareth the rod
hateth his son."

Husband: It must be time to get up.
Wife: How can you tell?
Husband: The baby has fallen asleep at last.

Coed: Daddy, the girl who sits next to me in
class has a dress just like mine.
Dad: So you want a new dress?
Coed: Well, it would be cheaper than changing
colleges.

Jed: Your sister is spoiled, isn't she?
Ted: No, that's the perfume she uses.

❖ ❖ ❖

Billy was in a store with his mother when he was given a stick of candy by one of the clerks.

"What do you say, Billy?" prompted his mother.

"Charge it!" he replied.

❖ ❖ ❖

The mother said firmly, "If you two boys can't agree and be quiet, I shall take your pie away."

The younger one replied, "But, Mother, we do agree. Bill wants the biggest piece, and so do I!"

❖ ❖ ❖

Mother: Eat your spinach. It will put color in your cheeks.
Son: Who wants green cheeks?

❖ ❖ ❖

There was an earthquake recently that frightened the inhabitants of a certain town. One couple sent their little boy to stay with an uncle in another district, explaining the reason for the nephew's sudden visit. A day later the parents received this telegram, "Am returning your boy. Send the earthquake."

❖ ❖ ❖

Johnny: Will I get everything I pray for, Mama?
Mother: Everything that's good for you, dear.
Johnny: Oh, what's the use, then? I get that
  anyway.

❖ ❖ ❖

"Mother, do give me another piece of sugar,"
little Helen requested.

"But you've had three already," her mother
pointed out.

"Just one more, please."

"Well, this must be the last."

"Thank you, Mother . . . but I must say, you
have no willpower."

❖ ❖ ❖

Auntie: When I was a child, I was told if I made
  ugly faces I would stay like that.
Little Joan: Well, you can't say you weren't
  warned, Auntie.

❖ ❖ ❖

Little boy to departing relative: There's no hurry,
  Uncle. Daddy has put the clock a whole hour
  ahead.

❖ ❖ ❖

Bobby had been to a birthday party, and, knowing his weakness, his mother looked him straight in the eyes and said, "I hope you didn't ask for a second piece of cake."

"No," replied Bobby. "I only asked Mrs. Jones for the recipe so you could make some like it, and she gave me two more pieces of her own accord."

❖ ❖ ❖

Little boy (calling father at office): Hello, who is this?

Father (recognizing son's voice): The smartest man in the world.

Little boy: Pardon me; I must have the wrong number.

❖ ❖ ❖

Father: Can you support her in the way she's accustomed to?

Prospective son-in-law: No, I can't support her in the manner she has been accustomed to, but I can support her in the way her mother was accustomed to when she was first married.

❖ ❖ ❖

Son: Dad, what is a weapon?
Father: Why, son, that's something you fight
   with.
Son: Is mother your weapon?

❖ ❖ ❖

A little boy never said a word for six years.
One day his parents served him cocoa. From out
of left field the kid says, "This cocoa's no good."
His parents went around raving. They said to
him, "Why did you wait so long to talk?" He
said, "Up till now everything's been okay."

❖ ❖ ❖

Father: Don't you think our son gets all his
   brains from me?
Mother: Probably. I still have all mine.

❖ ❖ ❖

Parents spend the first part of a child's life
urging him to walk and talk, and the rest of his
childhood making him sit down and keep quiet.

❖ ❖ ❖

A third grader went home and told her
mother she was in love with a classmate and
was going to marry him.

"That's fine," said her mother, going along with the gag. "Does he have a job?"

The little girl replied, "Oh, yes. He erases the blackboard in our class."

❖ ❖ ❖

Summertime is when parents pack off their troubles to an old Indian Camp and smile, smile, smile!

❖ ❖ ❖

Visitor: Does your baby brother talk yet?
Freddy: He doesn't have to. He gets everything he wants by yelling.

❖ ❖ ❖

My boy is 15 . . . going on 12!

❖ ❖ ❖

"You look pretty dirty, Susie."
"Thank you. I look pretty when I'm clean, too."

❖ ❖ ❖

A message for all parents: Is your teenage son or daughter out for the evening? If so, take advantage of the opportunity. Pack your furniture, call a moving van, and don't leave a forwarding address.

❖ ❖ ❖

Nothing annoys a woman more than to have friends drop in unexpectedly and find the house looking as it usually does.

❖ ❖ ❖

Mother: How could you be so rude and tell your sister she's stupid? Tell her you're sorry.
Boy: Sis, I'm sorry you're stupid!

❖ ❖ ❖

On his first visit to the zoo, a little boy stared at the caged stork for a long while. Then he turned to his father and exclaimed, "Gee, Dad, he doesn't recognize me."

❖ ❖ ❖

"Young man, there were two cookies in the pantry this morning. May I ask how it happens that there is only one now?"
"Must have been so dark I didn't see the other one."

❖ ❖ ❖

Boy: Dad, I just got a part in the school play. I play the part of a man who's been married for 25 years.

Father: That's a good start, son. Just keep right at it and one of these days you'll get a speaking part!

❖ ❖ ❖

Boy: Mom, Dad just backed the car out of the garage and ran over my bicycle.
Mother: Serves you right, son, for leaving it on the front lawn.

❖ ❖ ❖

A six-year-old ran up and down the supermarket aisles shouting frantically, "Marian, Marian."

Finally reunited with his mother, he was chided by her, "You shouldn't call me 'Marian.' I'm your mother, you know."

"I know," he replied, "but the store is full of mothers."

❖ ❖ ❖

Father: Son, do you realize when Lincoln was your age he was already studying hard to be a lawyer?
Son: Right, Pop, and when he was your age, he was already president of the United States!

❖ ❖ ❖

A man in a supermarket was pushing a cart that contained, among other things, a screaming baby. As the man proceeded along the aisles, he kept repeating softly, "Keep calm, George. Don't get excited, George. Don't yell, George."

A lady watched with admiration and then said, "You are certainly to be commended for your patience in trying to quiet little George."

"Lady," he declared, "I'm George!"

❖ ❖ ❖

I know a teenage girl who has been trying to run away from home for a year but every time she gets to the front door the phone rings.

20

Marriage

The best way for a man to remember his wife's birthday is to forget it just once.

❖ ❖ ❖

Views expressed by husbands are not necessarily those of the management.

❖ ❖ ❖

A lot of husbands have an impediment in their speech. Every time they open their mouth the wife interrupts.

❖ ❖ ❖

In my house, I make all the major decisions and my wife makes the minor ones. For example, I decide such things as East–West trade, crime in the streets, welfare cheating, and increases in taxes. My wife decides the minor things such as which house to buy, what kind of car we drive, how much money to spend, and how to raise the children.

❖ ❖ ❖

Being a husband is like any other job. It helps a lot if you like the boss.

❖ ❖ ❖

You can always tell when a marriage is shaky. The partners don't even talk to each other during television commercials.

❖ ❖ ❖

Announcement: The lodge meeting will be postponed. The Supreme Exalted Invincible Unlimited Sixty-Ninth Degree Potentate's wife wouldn't let him come!

❖ ❖ ❖

Marriage is like a midnight phone call. You get a ring and then you wake up.

❖ ❖ ❖

It has been proven that married life is healthy. Statistics show that single people die sooner than married folks. So, if you're looking for a long life and a slow death, get married!

❖ ❖ ❖

Marriage counselor to wife: "Maybe your problem is that you've been waking up grumpy in the morning."

"No, I always let him sleep."

❖ ❖ ❖

A newly married couple were entertaining, and among the guests was a man whose conduct was rather boisterous. At dinner he held up on his fork a piece of meat and, in an attempt at humor, asked: "Is this pig?"

"To which end of the fork do you refer?" asked a quiet-looking man at the other end of the table.

❖ ❖ ❖

The honeymoon is over when he no longer smiles gently as he scrapes the burnt toast.

❖ ❖ ❖

A new group of male applicants had just arrived in heaven. Peter looked them over and ordered, "All men who were henpecked on earth, please step to the left; all those who were bosses in their own homes, step to the right."

The line quickly formed on the left. Only one man stepped to the right.

Peter looked at the frail little man standing by himself and inquired, "What makes you think you belong on this side?"

Without hesitation the meek little man explained, "Because this is where my wife told me to stand."

✧ ✧ ✧

The cooing usually stops when the honeymoon is over, but the billing goes on forever.

✧ ✧ ✧

A married couple trying to live up to a snobbish lifestyle went to a party. The conversation turned to Mozart, "Absolutely brilliant . . . lovely . . . oh, a fine fellow . . . a genius, Mozart."

The woman, wanting to join in the general conversation, remarked casually, "Ah, Mozart. You're so right. I love him. Only this morning I saw him getting on the No. 5 bus going to Coney Island."

There was a sudden hush and everyone looked at her. Her husband was shattered. He pulled her away. "We're leaving right now. Get your coat and come."

In the car as they drove home, he kept muttering to himself. Finally, his wife turned to him.

"You are angry about something."

"Oh, really? You noticed it?" he sneered. "My goodness! I've never been so embarrassed in my life! You saw Mozart take the No. 5 bus to Coney Island? Don't you know the No. 5 bus doesn't go to Coney Island?"

❖ ❖ ❖

He was escorting his wife to a concert and they arrived late. "What are they playing?" he whispered to his neighbor.

"The Fifth Symphony," replied the man.

"Well, thank goodness," sighed the husband. "I've missed four of them."

❖ ❖ ❖

A Kansas cyclone hit a farmhouse just before dawn one morning. It lifted the roof off, picked up the beds on which the farmer and his wife slept, and set them down gently in the next county.

The wife began to cry.

"Don't be scared, Mary," her husband said. "We're not hurt."

Mary continued to cry. "I'm not scared," she responded between sobs. "I'm happy 'cause this is the first time in 14 years we've been out together."

❖ ❖ ❖

"Was your husband outspoken?"
"Not by anyone I know of."

❖ ❖ ❖

"Did your wife have much to say when you got home last night?"

"No, but that didn't keep her from talking for two hours."

❖ ❖ ❖

Wife: Scientists claim that the average person speaks 10,000 words a day.
Husband: Yes, dear, but remember, you are far above average.

❖ ❖ ❖

Wife: This is rabbit stew we're having.
Husband: Thought so. I just found a hair in mine.

❖ ❖ ❖

Whenever my wife needs money, she calls me handsome. She says, "Hand some over."

❖ ❖ ❖

There are only two ways to handle a woman—and nobody knows either of them.

❖ ❖ ❖

Some people ask the secret of our long marriage. We take time to go to a restaurant two times a week. A little candlelight, dinner, soft

music, and a slow walk home. She goes
Tuesdays; I go Fridays.

And speaking about all the marriages of
high-school kids, one elderly gent of 20 swore he
attended one wedding ceremony where the
groom wept for two hours. It seems the bride
got a bigger piece of cake than he did.

Despite the statistics, he denies that married
men live longer than single men . . . it only
seems longer.

One thing I'll say for my wife, she's a very
neat housekeeper. If I drop my socks on the
floor, she picks them up. If I throw my clothes
around, she hangs them up. I got up at 3 o'clock
the other morning, went into the kitchen to get a
glass of orange juice. I came back and found the
bed made.

A man and his wife were returning to their
seats after a movie intermission. In a voice of
concern, he asked a man at the end of a row,
"Did I step on your toes on the way out?"

"You certainly did," responded the other angrily.

"All right," he said, turning to his wife. "This is our row."

❖ ❖ ❖

Wife: Honey, I can't get the car started. I think it's flooded.
Husband: Where is it?
Wife: In the swimming pool.
Husband: It's flooded.

❖ ❖ ❖

Husband: Where is yesterday's newspaper?
Wife: I wrapped the garbage in it.
Husband: Oh, I wanted to see it.
Wife: There wasn't much to see . . . just some orange peels and coffee grounds.

❖ ❖ ❖

Husband: Janice, when I see you in that hat, I laugh.
Wife: Good! I'll put it on when the bill comes in.

❖ ❖ ❖

"I wonder if my husband will love me when my hair is gray?"

"Why not? He's loved you through three shades already."

❖ ❖ ❖

She's an angel . . . always up in the air and harping on things.

❖ ❖ ❖

Wife: I just got back from the beauty shop.
Husband: What's the matter? Was it closed?

❖ ❖ ❖

A young man came home from the office and found his bride sobbing convulsively. "I feel terrible," she told him. "I was pressing your suit and I burned a big hole right in the seat of your trousers."

"Forget it," consoled her husband. "Remember that I've got an extra pair of pants for that suit."

"Yes, and it's lucky you have," said the woman, drying her eyes. "I used them to patch the hole."

❖ ❖ ❖

"Hello, Sam," exclaimed Jim, meeting a buddy for the first time since the war's end. "Did you marry that girl you used to go with or are you still doing your own cooking and ironing?"

"Yes," replied Sam.

❖ ❖ ❖

A couple, just married, got among their wedding presents two tickets to a very fine show, with the notation "Guess who" on the tickets. They went to the play. When they returned, all of their wedding presents were gone, and a note was left "Now you know!"

❖ ❖ ❖

A sorely pressed newlywed sought valiantly to console his bride, who was crying on the sofa.

"Darling," he implored, "believe me. I never said you were a terrible cook. I merely pointed out that our garbage disposal has developed an ulcer."

❖ ❖ ❖

Wife: You both arrived at that cab at the same time. Why did you let him have it? Why didn't you stand up for your rights?
Husband: He needed it more than I did. He was late to his karate class.

❖ ❖ ❖

He: Will you love me when I am old and wrinkled?
She: Yes, I do!

❖ ❖ ❖

Wife: When we were younger, you used to
    nibble on my ear.
(The husband starts to leave the room.)
Wife: Where are you going?
Husband: To get my teeth!

❖ ❖ ❖

"But, my dear," protested the henpecked
husband, "I've done nothing. You've been talking for an hour and a half and I haven't said a
word."

"I know," the wife replied. "But you listen
like a wise guy."

❖ ❖ ❖

Wife: Look at the old clothes I have to wear. If
    people came to visit, they would think I was
    the cook!
Husband: Well, they'd change their minds if
    they stayed for dinner!

❖ ❖ ❖

Wife: George! Come quickly! A wild tiger has
    just gone into mother's tent!
Husband: Well, he got himself into that mess; let
    him get himself out of it!

❖ ❖ ❖

Wife: Darling, you know that cake you asked me to bake for you? Well, the dog ate it.
Husband: That's okay, dear. Don't cry. I'll buy you another dog!

❖ ❖ ❖

"My wife spent four hours in the beauty shop the other day."
"Boy, that's a long time."
"Yeah, and that was just for the estimate!"

❖ ❖ ❖

Wife: I dreamed you gave me $100 for summer clothes last night. You wouldn't spoil that dream, would you, dear?
Husband: Of course not, darling. You may keep the $100.

My husband really embarrassed me the other day in a restaurant. When he drank his soup, six couples got up and started to dance.

❖ ❖ ❖

Husband: Where did you get that new hat?
Wife: Don't worry, dear. It didn't cost a thing. It was marked down from $20 to $10. So, I bought it with the $10 I saved.

21

Medicine

Doctor: Well, your leg is swollen, but I wouldn't
worry about it.
Patient: No, and if your leg was swollen I
wouldn't worry about it either.

❖ ❖ ❖

First doctor: Have you ever made a serious mistake in the diagnosis of a patient?
Second doctor: Yes, I once treated a patient for
indigestion when he could have afforded an
appendectomy.

❖ ❖ ❖

A man sought medical aid because he had
popped eyes and a ringing in the ears. A doctor
looked him over and suggested removal of his
tonsils. The operation resulted in no improvement, so the patient consulted another doctor

who suggested removal of his teeth. The teeth were extracted but still the man's eyes popped and the ringing in his ears continued.

A third doctor told him bluntly, "You've got six months to live."

In that event, the doomed man decided he'd treat himself right while he could. He bought a flashy car, hired a chauffeur, had the best tailor in town make him 30 suits. Then he decided that even his shirts would be made-to-order.

"Okay," said the shirtmaker, "let's get your measurement. Hmm, 34 sleeve, 16 collar—"

"Fifteen" the man said.

"Sixteen collar," the shirtmaker repeated, measuring again.

"But I've always worn a 15 collar," said the man.

"Listen," the shirtmaker said, "I'm warning you. You keep on wearing a 15 collar and your eyes will pop and you'll have ringing in your ears."

❖ ❖ ❖

Patient: What are your fees, doctor?

Doctor: I charge ten dollars for the first visit and five dollars for the second visit.

Patient: Well, doctor, it's nice to see you again! What should I do?

Doctor: Take the same medicine I gave you last time.

❖ ❖ ❖

Doctor: Say, the check you gave me for my doctor bill came back.
Patient: So did my arthritis.

❖ ❖ ❖

"What are you taking for your cold?"
"I don't know. What will you give me?"

❖ ❖ ❖

His psychiatrist just told him, "You haven't got an inferiority complex. You are inferior."

❖ ❖ ❖

Patient: Doctor, it's 2 A.M. and I can't sleep. It's the bill I owe you. I can't pay it. It bothers me so much I can't sleep.
Doctor: Why did you have to tell me that? Now I can't sleep.

❖ ❖ ❖

Doctor: I see you're coughing better this morning.
Patient: Why not? I've been practicing all night.

❖ ❖ ❖

Talk about children mimicking their parents! I understand Hollywood kids don't play doctor

and nurse anymore. It's psychiatrist and neurotic!

✧ ✧ ✧

Mrs. Jones was suddenly taken ill in the
night, and a new doctor was called to the house.
After a look at the patient, the doctor stepped
outside the sickroom to ask Mr. Jones for a
corkscrew. Given the tool, he disappeared but
several minutes later was back demanding a
pair of pliers. Again he disappeared into the
room of the moaning patient, only to call out
again, "A chisel and mallet, quick!"

Mr. Jones could stand it no longer. "What is
her trouble, doctor?"

"Don't know yet," was the reply. "I can't get
my instrument bag open."

✧ ✧ ✧

A man pleaded with the psychiatrist, "You've
got to help me. It's my son."

"What's the matter?"

"He's always eating mud pies. I get up in the
morning and there he is in the backyard eating
mud pies. I come home at lunch and he is eating
mud pies. I come home at dinner and there he is
in the backyard eating mud pies."

The psychiatrist reassured him, "Give the
kid a chance. It's all part of growing up. It'll
pass."

"Well, I don't like it—and neither does his wife."

❖ ❖ ❖

The latest thing in psychiatry is group therapy. Instead of couches, they use bunk beds.

❖ ❖ ❖

Two psychiatrists met on the street. One smiled brightly and said, "Good morning!" The other walked on and muttered to himself, "I wonder what he meant by that!"

❖ ❖ ❖

Dentist: What kind of filling would you like in your tooth?
Boy: Chocolate!

❖ ❖ ❖

George was having trouble with a toothache, so he decided to visit the dentist.

"What do you charge for extracting a tooth?" George asked.

"Fifty dollars," replied the dentist.

"Fifty dollars for only two minutes of work!" exclaimed George.

"Well," replied the dentist, "if you wish, I can extract it very slowly."

❖ ❖ ❖

Doctor: I have some good news and some bad
news. Which do you want first?
Patient: Give me the bad news first.
Doctor: We amputated the wrong leg.
Patient: What is the good news?
Doctor: Your other leg won't need to be ampu-
tated after all.

❖ ❖ ❖

Surgeons invited to dinner parties are often
asked to carve the meat—or worse yet, to watch
the host carve while commenting on the surgeon's occupation. At one part, a surgeon friend
was watching the carving while his host kept up
a running commentary: "How am I doing, doc?
How do you like that technique? I'd make a
pretty good surgeon, don't you think?"

When the host finished and the slices of
meat lay neatly on the serving platter, the surgeon spoke up: "Anybody can take them apart,
Harry. Now let's see you put them back together
again."

❖ ❖ ❖

"I had an operation and the doctor left a
sponge in me."

"Got any pain?"
"No, but boy do I ever get thirsty!"

✧ ✧ ✧

He always feels bad when he feels good for fear he'll feel worse when he feels better.

✧ ✧ ✧

Inscription on the tombstone of a hypochondriac: "Now will you believe I'm sick?"

✧ ✧ ✧

Patient: My right foot hurts.
Doctor: It's just old age.
Patient: But my left foot is just as old. How come it doesn't hurt?

✧ ✧ ✧

He's so full of penicillin that every time he sneezes he cures a dozen people.

✧ ✧ ✧

He is such a hypochondriac he won't even talk on the phone to anyone who has a cold.

✧ ✧ ✧

She is a very fine doctor. If you can't afford the operation, she touches up the X-rays.

✧ ✧ ✧

Doctors keep telling us to get lots of fresh air, but they never tell us where to find it.

✧ ✧ ✧

Did you hear about the poor fellow who told his doctor he heard music every time he put his hat on? The doctor fixed him right up. He took the guy's hat and removed the band.

✧ ✧ ✧

Did you hear about the man who swallowed his glass eye and was rushed to a stomach specialist? The specialist peered down the unfortunate fellow's throat and exclaimed, "I've looked into a lot of stomachs in my day, but I must say, this is the first one that ever looked back at me."

✧ ✧ ✧

Two women went to the movies, and one of them started to cough. Her friend leaned away from her. The more she coughed, the farther her friend tried to move away. Finally, the cougher turned around to her friend and said, "Look, you don't have to move away like that. This is not a sickness."

Her friend replied, "Well, it isn't a wellness."

✧ ✧ ✧

"Doctor, will I be able to read with these new glasses?"

"Yes, of course."

"Good! I never could read before."

✧ ✧ ✧

"I've been seeing spots in front of my eyes."

"Have you seen a doctor?"

"No, just spots."

✧ ✧ ✧

Looking down at the sick man, the doctor decided to tell him the truth. "I feel I should tell you that you are a very sick man. I'm sure you would want to know the facts. I don't think you have much time left. Is there anyone you would like to see right now?"

Bending down toward his patient, the doctor heard him feebly answer, "Yes."

"Who is it?"

In a slightly stronger tone, the sufferer said, "Another doctor."

✧ ✧ ✧

I won't say he's neurotic, but last week he was watching the Army–Navy game on television, and every time one of the teams went into a huddle he wondered if they were talking about him.

Now they've got a tranquilizer atomizer . . . one spray and it calms you down to the point where you can take a pill.

❖ ❖ ❖

I went to my doctor last week and she told me to take a hot bath before retiring. But that's ridiculous! It'll be years before I retire!

❖ ❖ ❖

When I got the bill for my operation, I found out why they wear masks in the operating room.

❖ ❖ ❖

A violinist was advised by the surgeon that he'd have to undergo an operation.

"But, doctor, intoned the patient, "I have concerts booked ahead. If you operate, can I be assured that I'll be able to play the violin in two weeks' time?"

"Undoubtedly!" assured the doctor, "The last patient on whom I performed this operation was playing a harp within 24 hours!"

❖ ❖ ❖

My arm started to hurt me so I asked the doctor to examine it. She looked at my arm and brought out a medical book and studied it for 15 minutes. The she said to me, "Have you ever had that pain before?" I said, "Yes." She said, "Well, you've got it again."

❖ ❖ ❖

Mr. Jones phoned the doctor for an appointment. The nurse said she could give him an appointment in two weeks.

"In two weeks I could be dead!" wailed Jones.

"Well, in that case," answered the nurse, "you can always cancel the appointment!"

❖ ❖ ❖

A doctor had a problem with a leak in his bathroom plumbing that became bigger and bigger. Even though it was 2 A.M., the doctor decided to phone his plumber.

"For Pete's sake, Doc," the plumber wailed, "this is some time to wake a guy."

"Well," the doctor answered testily, "you've never hesitated to call me in the middle of the night with a medical problem. Now it just happens I've got a plumbing emergency."

There was a moment's silence. Then the plumber spoke up, "Right you are, Doc," he agreed. "Tell me what's wrong."

The doctor explained about the leak in the bathroom.

"I'll tell you what to do," the plumber offered. "Take two aspirins every four hours and drop them down the pipe. If the leak hasn't cleared up by morning, phone me at the office."

Sam: Why do doctors and nurses wear masks?
Pete: So that if someone makes a mistake no one will know who did it.

The doctor told me to take this medicine after a hot bath. I could hardly finish drinking the bath!

22

Miscellaneous

"I caught a 250-pound marlin the other day!"

"That's nothing. I was fishing and hooked a lamp from an old Spanish ship. In fact, the light was still lit!"

"If you will blow out the light, I'll take 200 pounds off the marlin!"

❖ ❖ ❖

A lawyer sent an overdue bill to a client with a note that said, "This bill is one year old."

By return mail the lawyer had his bill back. To it was attached another note: "Happy Birthday."

❖ ❖ ❖

❖ ❖ ❖

"How do you know your family was poor?"

"Every time I passed someone in town, they would say, 'There goes Joe. His poor family . . .'"

❖ ❖ ❖

It is not always easy to say the right thing on the spur of the moment. We can sympathize with the chap who met an old friend after many years.

"How is your wife?"

"She is in heaven," replied the friend.

"Oh, I'm sorry," stammered the chap. Then he realized this was not the thing to say. "I mean," he stammered, "I'm glad." That seemed even worse so he blurted, "Well, what I really mean is, I'm surprised."

❖ ❖ ❖

Shoe salesman who had dragged out half his stock to a woman customer: Mind if I rest a few minutes, lady? Your feet are killing me.

❖ ❖ ❖

Bus driver: Are you enjoying the bus ride?

Male passenger: Yes!

Bus driver: Then why are you riding with your eyes shut?

Male passenger: I'm okay. It's just that I hate to see women stand!

❖ ❖ ❖

"What did your husband get you for your birthday?"

"A smog device."

"Why a smog device?"

"He said my breath was a major cause of air pollution."

❖ ❖ ❖

Newsboy: Extra, extra! Read all about it—two men swindled.

Man: Give me one. Say, there isn't anything about two men being swindled.

Newsboy: Extra, extra! Three men swindled.

❖ ❖ ❖

"What are you doing?"

"I'm watering my beans."

"But there is no water coming out of the can."

"Do you see any beans?"

❖ ❖ ❖

"Say, mister, would you give me a dollar for a sandwich?"

"I dunno. Lemme see the sandwich!"

❖ ❖ ❖

"Did you take a bath today?"

"Why? Is one missing?"

❖ ❖ ❖

Woman: I would like a pair of alligator shoes.
Man: Yes, ma'am. What size is your alligator?

❖ ❖ ❖

"You're the laziest man I ever saw. Don't you do anything quickly?"
"Yes, I get tired fast."

❖ ❖ ❖

"I can't pay the rent this month."
"But you said that last month."
"I kept my word, didn't I?"

❖ ❖ ❖

"Have any big men ever been born in this town?"
"No, just little babies."

❖ ❖ ❖

"Mr. Editor, do you think I should put more fire into my stories?"
"No, just the opposite."

❖ ❖ ❖

A man was waiting at an intersection for a circus to pass by. He saw a sign on one of the wagons that read: "Barney's Circus with 50 Elephants." He counted the elephants as they crossed the intersection. When he got to 50, he put his car in gear and started to cross the intersection because he was late for an appointment. Unfortunately, he had miscounted and his car hit and killed the last elephant.

A week later he got a notice from the circus that he'd have to pay $1,000,000. He called the circus manager and inquired, "What's the deal? I only hit one lousy elephant! Why do you want $1,000,000?"

The manager responded, "It's true, you only hit one elephant but you pulled the tails out of 49 others!"

❖ ❖ ❖

Did you hear about the spinster who couldn't see too well? In order to hide her failing eyesight from her intended, she stuck a pin in a tree. The next day, while walking in the forest with him, she pointed to the tree, some hundred yards distant, and said, "Isn't that a pin sticking in that tree?" But as she ran to retrieve it, she tripped over a cow.

❖ ❖ ❖

A man put a coin in a vending machine and watched helplessly while the cup failed to appear. One nozzle sent coffee down the drain while another poured cream after it.

"Now that's real automation!" he exclaimed. "It even drinks for you!"

✧ ✧ ✧

Two men were digging a ditch on a very hot day. One said to the other, "Why are we down in this hole digging a ditch when our boss is standing up there in the shade of a tree?"

"I don't know," responded the other. "I'll ask him."

So he climbed out of the hole and went to his boss. "Why are we digging in the hot sun and you're standing in the shade?"

"Intelligence," the boss said.

"What do you mean, 'intelligence'?"

The boss said, "Well, I'll show you. I'll put my hand on this tree and I want you to hit it with your fist as hard as you can."

The ditch-digger took a mighty swing and tried to hit the boss' hand. The boss removed his hand and the ditch-digger hit the tree. The boss said, "That's intelligence!"

The ditch-digger went back to his hole. His friend asked, "What did he say?"

"He said we are down here because of intelligence."

"What's intelligence?" said the friend. The ditch-digger put his hand on his face and said, "Take your shovel and hit my hand."

✧ ✧ ✧

The inmates of a prison had a joke book they all had memorized. The way they recited them was by the number of the joke. Some fellow would call out a number from 1 to 100 and all would laugh.

A new man in the prison, after studying the book, said he wanted to tell a joke. They said, "O.K., shoot!"

He said, "Number 20," but nobody laughed. He said, "This is funny. What's wrong? Why aren't you laughing?"

A fellow nearby said, "Some can tell them and some can't."

✧ ✧ ✧

A village blacksmith working at his open forge hammering a white-hot horseshoe had just finished the shoe and thrown it to the ground to cool.

The local wise guy walked in at that moment. He picked up the horseshoe, but dropped it with a howl of pain.

"Pretty hot, eh?" asked the blacksmith.

"Naw," said the wise guy. "It just doesn't take me long to look over a horseshoe."

❖ ❖ ❖

An old miser, because of his exceptional thrift, had no friends. Just before he died he asked his doctor, lawyer, and minister to gather around his bedside.

"I have always heard you can't take it with you, but I am going to prove you can," he said. "I have $90,000 in cash under my mattress. It's in three envelopes of $30,000 each. I want each of you to take one envelope now and just before they throw the dirt on me you throw the envelopes in."

The three attended the funeral and each threw his envelope into the grave. On the way back from the cemetery, the minister said, "I don't feel exactly right. I'm going to confess. I needed $10,000 badly for a new church we are building, so I took out $10,000 and threw only $20,000 in the grave."

The doctor said, "I, too, must confess. I am building a hospital and took $20,000 and threw in only $10,000."

The lawyer said, "Gentlemen, I'm surprised, shocked, and ashamed of you. I don't see how you could hold out that money. I threw in my personal check for the full amount."

❖ ❖ ❖

A hunter shot a duck and it fell into the lake. Quickly, he commanded his dog—a dog he'd never worked before—to retrieve. The bird dog ran to the edge of the water, sniffed, then walked out onto the waters of the lake. The hunter was amazed. He shot another duck. It, too, fell into the lake. Again the dog walked out on the water to retrieve the duck before it sank. *At last,* the hunter thought, *I have something to show that friend of mine who never lets anything get to him.*

The next day the hunter suggested to his friend that they do a little duck hunting. His friend shot a duck, and it fell into the lake. The dog walked across the water to retrieve it and dropped it at the shooter's feet.

The hunter asked his friend, "What do you think of my bird dog? Did you notice anything special about him?"

"I noticed one thing: He can't swim!"

❖ ❖ ❖

I now have 180 books but I don't have a bookcase . . . nobody will lend me one!

❖ ❖ ❖

"I'm not a liar, sir. I just remember big."

❖ ❖ ❖

If the garbage workers in your community ever go out on strike, you might like to know how a wise New Yorker disposed of his refuse for the nine days the sanitation workers were off the job last summer. Each day he wrapped his garbage in gift paper. Then he put it in a shopping bag. When he parked his car, he left the bag on the front seat with the window open. When he got back to the car, the garbage had always been collected.

When some people retire, nobody knows the difference.

A man seldom makes the same mistake twice. Generally, it's three times or more.

"Oh! Oh! I'm hit!"
"You shot bad, Tex?"
"You ever hear of anyone being shot good?"

Joe and Bill met on a street corner. When Joe said he sure was glad to see his friend, Bill answered, "How can you see me when I'm not even here? And I'll bet you $10 I can prove it!"
"You're going to bet me $10 you're not here? Okay, it's a bet. Go ahead and prove it."

"Am I in Chicago?"

"Nope."

"Am I in New York?"

Joe answered emphatically, "No!"

"Well, if I'm not in Chicago and I'm not in New York, that means I'm in some other place, right?"

"That's right."

"Well, if I'm in some other place, I can't be here. I'll take that $10."

"How can I give you the money if you're not here?" Joe replied.

❖ ❖ ❖

A man dropped in to pay a friend an unexpected visit and was amazed to find him playing chess with a dog. The man watched in silence for a few minutes, then burst out with, "That's the most incredible dog I ever saw in my life!"

"Oh, he isn't so smart," was the answer. "I've beaten him three games out of four."

❖ ❖ ❖

"I haven't slept for days."

"How come?"

"I only sleep at night."

❖ ❖ ❖

An elderly widower loved his cat so dearly he tried to teach it to talk. "If I can get Tabby to converse with me," he reasoned, "I won't have to bother with ornery humans at all." First, he tried a diet of canned salmon, then one of canaries. Tabby obviously approved of both but he didn't learn to talk. Then one day the widower had two parrots cooked in butter and served to Tabby with asparagus and french fries. Tabby licked the plate clean, and then . . . wonder of wonders . . . suddenly turned to her master and shouted, "Look out!"

Possibly the widower didn't hear because he never moved a muscle. The next moment the ceiling caved in and buried him under a mass of debris. The cat shook its head and said in disgust, "Eight years he spends getting me to talk, and then the idiot doesn't listen."

❖ ❖ ❖

In front of a delicatessen, an art connoisseur noticed a mangy little kitten lapping up milk from a saucer. The saucer, he realized with a start, was a rare and precious piece of pottery.

He sauntered into the store and offered two dollars for the cat.

"It's not for sale," said the proprietor.

"Look," said the collector, "that cat is dirty and undesirable, but I'm eccentric. I like cats that way. I'll raise my offer to five dollars."

"It's a deal," said the proprietor, and pocketed the five spot.

"For that sum I'm sure you won't mind throwing in the saucer," said the connoisseur. "The kitten seems so happy drinking from it."

"Nothing doing," said the proprietor firmly. "That's my lucky saucer. From that saucer so far this week, I've sold 34 cats."

✧ ✧ ✧

Creditors have better memories than debtors.

✧ ✧ ✧

A farmer had a wife who was very critical of his vocabulary. One evening he told her he had a friend named Bill he would like her to meet.

"Don't call him 'Bill,' " she insisted. "Call him 'William.' "

When the friend arrived, the farmer said, "Let me tell you a tale."

"Not tale," the wife interrupted. "Say, 'anecdote.' "

That night, upon retiring, the farmer told her to put out the light.

"Not 'put out,' " she exclaimed, "Say, 'extinguish.' "

Later in the night she awakened her husband and sent him downstairs to investigate a noise. When he returned, she asked him what it was.

"It was," he explained carefully, "a William goat which I took by its anecdote and extinguished."

❖ ❖ ❖

"Those are fighting words where I come from!"

"Well, why don't you fight then?"

" 'Cause I ain't where I come from."

❖ ❖ ❖

"What a lot of friends we lose through their borrowing money from us."

"Yes, it is touch and go with most of them."

❖ ❖ ❖

A Texan was visiting Scotland and every time his host would show him a sight he would say, "That's nothing! We've got the same thing in Texas, only better!"

Finally they arrived at Loch Lomond. The Texan said, "Well, you have one thing that we don't have in Texas. This is a pretty lake."

The host said, "Well, you could dig a pipeline from Texas under the ocean and into the lake. And if you can suck as hard as you can blow, the lake is yours."

❖ ❖ ❖

Lady: Oh, isn't he sweet. Little boy, if you give me a kiss, I'll give you a bright new penny.

Little boy: I get twice as much at home for just taking cough medicine.

❖ ❖ ❖

Mark Twain once encountered a friend at the races who said, "I'm broke. I wish you'd buy me a ticket back to town."

Twain said, "Well, I'm pretty broke myself, but I'll tell you what to do. You hide under my seat, and I'll cover you with my legs." It was agreed. Twain then went to the ticket office and bought two tickets. When the train was underway and the supposed stowaway was snug under the seat, the conductor came by, and Twain gave him the two tickets.

"Where is the other passenger?" asked the conductor.

Twain tapped his forehead and said in a loud voice, "That is my friend's ticket. He's a little eccentric and likes to ride under the seat."

❖ ❖ ❖

Three polar bears were sitting on an iceberg. All were cold and quiet. Finally, the father bear said, "Now I've a tale to tell."

"I, too, have a tale to tell," said the mother bear.

The little polar bear looked up at his parents and said, "My tale is told!"

❖ ❖ ❖

My hotel room was so small the mice were hunchbacked.

❖ ❖ ❖

Judy: What did you do to your hair? It looks like a wig.
Joan: It is a wig.
Judy: You know? You could never tell!

A couple in Hollywood got divorced. Then they got remarried. The divorce didn't work.

❖ ❖ ❖

A man I know solved the problem of too many visiting relatives. He borrowed money from the rich ones and loaned it to the poor ones. Now none of them come back.

A gorilla walked into a drugstore and ordered a sundae. He put down a dollar bill to pay for it. The clerk thought, *What can a gorilla know about money?* So he handed back a single dollar in change.

As he did, he said, "You know, we don't get many gorillas in here."

"No wonder," answered the gorilla, "at 9 dollars a sundae."

✧ ✧ ✧

A newsman sent a letter home from China. At the end he put a note, "I hope this letter reaches you. The censors are very tough." When the letter arrived, another note had been added, "There are no censors in the People's Republic of China."

✧ ✧ ✧

Last night I dreamed I ate a five-pound marshmallow. When I woke up, my pillow was gone.

✧ ✧ ✧

Betty: I wish I had enough money to buy an elephant.
Joe: Why do you want an elephant?
Betty: I don't; I just want the money.

✧ ✧ ✧

Now for a couple of dillies: dilly, dilly.

✧ ✧ ✧

Blowhard: Did you hear the smartest kid in the world is becoming deaf?
Joe: No, tell me about it.
Blowhard: What did you say?

❖ ❖ ❖

A man tried to sell his neighbor a new dog. "This is a talking dog," he said. "And you can have him for five dollars."

The neighbor said, "Who do you think you're kidding with this talking dog stuff? There ain't no such animal."

Suddenly the dog looked up with tears in his eyes. "Please buy me, sir," he pleaded. "This man is cruel. He never buys me a meal, never bathes me, never takes me for a walk. And I used to be the richest trick dog in America. I performed before kings. I was in the Army and decorated ten times."

"Hey!" said the neighbor. "He can talk. Why do you want to sell him for just five dollars?"

"Because," said the seller, "I'm getting tired of all his lies."

❖ ❖ ❖

A fellow had been standing in line to get into a movie theater. He was surprised when he reached the box office because the price for the ticket was $6.50. He pointed to a sign that said "popular prices" and said, "You call $6.50 'popular'?"

"We like it," answered the woman sweetly

Two men were riding on a train for the first time. They brought bananas for lunch. Just as one of them bit into his banana, the train entered a tunnel.

First man: Did you take a bite of your banana?

Second man: No.

First man: Well, don't. I did and went blind!

✧ ✧ ✧

Sue: See that woman over there? She's been married four times . . . once to a millionaire; then to an actor; third, to a minister; and last to an undertaker.

Sal: I know! One for the money, two for the show, three to get ready, and four to go.

✧ ✧ ✧

And then there are people who claim movies would be better if they shot less film and more actors.

✧ ✧ ✧

Here it is in the middle of January and we're still cleaning up from Christmas. Last week we cleaned out our checking account; this week we cleaned out our savings account.

❖ ❖ ❖

So this man walks into a Fifth Avenue bank and says, "Pardon me, I'd like to talk with the fella that arranges loans."

The guard replied, "I'm sorry but the loan arranger is out to lunch."

"In that case, I'd like to talk to Tonto!"

❖ ❖ ❖

I used to box. My best punch was a rabbit punch, but they would never let me fight rabbits.

❖ ❖ ❖

Joe: Is that all there is to the story?
Joan: I guess so. I've already told you more than I heard.

❖ ❖ ❖

Did you hear about the undertaker who closes all his letters with "Eventually yours"?

❖ ❖ ❖

A little boy came home from school crying, "Mommy, Mommy, the kids at school called me a three-headed monster."

The mother responded sympathetically: "Now, there, there, there."

❖ ❖ ❖

I've discovered an easy way to get rich. You buy 50 female pigs and 50 male deer and put them together. Then you will have 100 sows and bucks.

❖ ❖ ❖

Remember the good old days when the still, small voice within us used to be called conscience instead of a radio?

❖ ❖ ❖

I understand the only people in the world who have no juvenile delinquency problems are the Eskimos . . . and it's all because of whale blubber. The minute a kid steps out of line they whale him 'till he blubbers!

❖ ❖ ❖

First cowboy: Why are you wearing only one spur?
Second cowboy: Well, I figure when one side of the horse starts running, the other side will too.

❖ ❖ ❖

Two kangaroos were talking to each other and one said, "I hope it doesn't rain today. I just hate it when the children play inside."

✧ ✧ ✧

I love Christmas. I receive a lot of presents I just can't wait to exchange.

✧ ✧ ✧

One time when my friend was in the breeding business, he crossed a parrot with a tiger. He doesn't know what it is, but when it talks everybody listens!

✧ ✧ ✧

Terry: Say something soft and sweet.
Jerry: Marshmallow.

✧ ✧ ✧

Stu: I guess my pen will just have to go on itching.
Sue: Why?
Stu: I'm all out of scratch paper.

✧ ✧ ✧

The only thing that keeps my house from falling down is that the termites are holding hands.

✧ ✧ ✧

"Knock, knock."
"Who's there?"
"Honeydew and cantaloupe."

"Honeydew and cantaloupe who?"

"Honeydew you love me? We cantaloupe now."

❖ ❖ ❖

"Knock, knock."

"Who's there?"

"Oswald."

"Oswald who?"

"Oswald mah gum."

❖ ❖ ❖

"Knock, knock."

"Who's there?"

"Divan."

"Divan who?"

"Divan the bathtub—I'm drowning."

❖ ❖ ❖

A weight-lifter was boasting about his strength and went on about it for some time. A gardener overheard and made him this offer: "Tell you what, I'll bet you $25 I can wheel a load in this wheelbarrow over there to the other side of the street that you can't wheel back."

"You're on," said Mr. Motormouth. "What's your load going to be?"

"Get in," said the gardener.

❖ ❖ ❖

Joe: Woman the lifeboats! Woman the lifeboats!
Moe: You don't "woman" the lifeboats. That's silly. You "man" the lifeboats!
Joe: You fill your lifeboats, and I'll fill mine.

❖ ❖ ❖

City slicker: Look at that bunch of cows.
Farmer: Not bunch . . . herd.
City slicker: Heard what?
Farmer: Herd of cows.
City slicker: Sure I've heard of cows.
Farmer: No, a cow herd.
City slicker: Why should I care what a cow heard? I've got no secrets from a cow.

❖ ❖ ❖

Joe: What kind of dog is that?
Blowhard: He's a police dog.
Joe: He sure doesn't look like one to me.
Blowhard: Of course not. He's an undercover cop.

❖ ❖ ❖

Guide showing a Texan Niagara Falls: I'll bet you don't have anything like that in Texas.
Texan: Nope, I reckon we don't. But we've got the plumbers who could fix it.

❖ ❖ ❖

Larry: You told me if I rubbed grease on my
    chest I'd grow tall like you, but it didn't work.
Harry: What did you use?
Larry: Crisco.
Harry: Stupid—that's shortening.

❖ ❖ ❖

A man who was late in paying his bills received
    the following note: "Your account has been on
    our books for over a year. Just want to remind
    you we have now carried you longer than
    your mother did."

❖ ❖ ❖

"I've invented a computer that's almost
human."
    "You mean, it can think?"
    "No. But when it makes a mistake it puts the
blame on another computer."

❖ ❖ ❖

A man was about to jump from the window
of a building when a passerby from the deep
South saw him and tried to talk him out of it.
    "For the sake of your mother, don't do it!"
the passerby pleaded.

"I don't have a mother."

"Well, think of your father."

"I don't have a father."

"Well, think of your wife."

"I never married."

"Well, then, think of Robert E. Lee!"

"Robert E. Lee? Who's he?"

"Never mind, Yankee. Go ahead and jump!"

❖ ❖ ❖

First reporter: What shall I say about the peroxide blondes who made such a fuss at the ball game?

Second reporter: Just say the bleachers went wild.

❖ ❖ ❖

"You shouldn't worry like that. It doesn't do any good."

"It does for me! Ninety percent of the things I worry about never happen!"

❖ ❖ ❖

"This house," said the real estate salesman, "has both its good points and its bad points. To show you I'm honest, I'm going to tell you about both. The disadvantages are that there is a chemical plant one block south and a slaughterhouse a block north."

"What are the advantages?" inquired the prospective buyer.

"The advantage is that you can always tell which way the wind is blowing."

✧ ✧ ✧

Joe: When I would wear my hand-me-downs to school, all the boys would make fun of me.
Moe: What did you do?
Joe: I hit them over the head with my purse!

✧ ✧ ✧

Did you hear about the farmer who decided to buy a chain saw? A logging foreman sold him one that he guaranteed would cut down 15 trees in a single day. A week later, a very unhappy farmer came back to report that the saw must be faulty—it averaged only three trees a day. The foreman grabbed the saw, pulled the cord, and the saw promptly went "Bzzzzzzz."

"Hey," demanded the startled farmer, "what's that noise?"

✧ ✧ ✧

Sign on wishing well: Wish Carefully. No Refunds.

✧ ✧ ✧

Mike: I always do my hardest work before breakfast.

Sandy: What's that?
Mike: Getting up.

❖ ❖ ❖

Did you hear about the new invention? A square bathtub! It eliminates the ring!

❖ ❖ ❖

"It took me all morning to fill this salt shaker."

"Why all morning?"

"It's hard to get the salt through those little holes on the top!"

❖ ❖ ❖

The smog was so bad in Los Angeles that I felt the sights and went back home!

❖ ❖ ❖

As they left the auditorium after a two-hour lecture on nineteenth-century English poets, the wife exclaimed, "Didn't it make your mind soar?"

"Yes," her husband agreed grimly, "and my backside, too!"

❖ ❖ ❖

A newspaper once carried an editorial that stated bluntly that half the city council were crooks. Under penalty of arrest, the editor issued the following retraction: "Half the city council aren't crooks."

❖ ❖ ❖

You can fool some of the people all of the time, and all of the people some of the time, but most of the time they will make fools of themselves.

❖ ❖ ❖

Red: Did you mark the place where the fishing was good?
Ted: Yes, I put an X on the side of the boat.
Red: That was stupid. What if we should take out another boat next time?

❖ ❖ ❖

There were three men in a boat halfway across a lake. The first man suddenly said, "I forgot my lunch," then got out of the boat and walked to shore on top of the water. Later, the second man said, "I forgot my fishing tackle" and also walked across the water to shore. By this time, the third man thought to himself, *They're not going to outsmart me.* "I forgot my bait can," he said and started to walk across the water . . . but he sank. The first man said to the second, "Maybe we should have told him where the rocks were."

On the Road

Sign on the Los Angeles boundary line: "You have just left the City of Los Angeles. Resume natural breathing."

✧ ✧ ✧

A motorist is a person who, after seeing a wreck, drives carefully for several blocks.

✧ ✧ ✧

Bud: All this talk about backseat driving is hogwash. I've driven for 15 years, and I've never heard a word from back there.
Dud: What kind of car do you drive?
Bud: A hearse.

✧ ✧ ✧

Nothing confuses a man more than driving behind a woman who does everything right!

❖ ❖ ❖

Those little cars have all kinds of advantages. Just this morning a motorcycle cop was chasing my Volkswagen. I knew I couldn't outrun him so I did the next best thing—drove up on the sidewalk and got lost in a crowd!

❖ ❖ ❖

I just solved the parking problem. I bought a parked car.

❖ ❖ ❖

There was a hitchhiker walking down the road. A young man drove up in a sports car and asked, "Do you want to race?"

So the hitchhiker started running and the young man speeded up to 60 MPH. When he looked back the hitchhiker was still in sight. The driver speeded up to 100 MPH and the hitchhiker was still running behind him. Then the driver speeded up to 120 MPH, and the hitchhiker disappeared from sight.

The driver decided to turn back and find the hitchhiker to see what happened. There was the hitchhiker lying exhausted in a ditch.

"What happened?" asked the driver.

"You'd blow out a tennis shoe, too, if you were going 120 MPH," said the hitchhiker.

❖ ❖ ❖

An insurance agent was teaching his wife to drive when the brakes suddenly failed on a steep, downhill grade.

"I can't stop!" she shrilled. "What should I do?"

"Brace yourself," advised her husband, "and try to hit something cheap."

❖ ❖ ❖

Angry customer: I thought you said this was a good car. It won't even go uphill.

Used car dealer: I said, "On the level, it's a fine car."

❖ ❖ ❖

A motorist had a flat tire in front of an insane asylum. He took the wheel off, and the bolts that held the wheel on rolled into the sewer.

A patient, looking through the fence, suggested that the man take one bolt from the remaining three wheels to hold the fourth wheel in place until he could get to a service station.

The motorist thanked him profusely and said, "I don't know why you are in that place."

The patient said, "I'm here for being crazy, not for being stupid."

❖ ❖ ❖

"I have a friend who is a real inventor. He took the fender from a Chevy, a motor from a Ford, and the transmission from a Sting Ray."

"Well, what did he get?"

"Three years."

❖ ❖ ❖

Did you hear about the cheerful truck driver who pulled up at a roadside cafe in the middle of the night for a dinner stop? Halfway through his dinner, three wild-looking motorcyclists roared up . . . bearded, leather-jacketed, filthy . . . with swastikas adorning their chests and helmets.

For no reason at all they selected the truck driver as a target. One poured pepper over his head, another stole his apple pie, the third deliberately upset his cup of coffee. The truck driver never said one word—just arose, paid his check, and exited.

"That trucker sure ain't much of a fighter," sneered one of the invaders.

The girl behind the counter, peering out into the night, added, "He doesn't seem to be much of a driver either. He just ran his truck right over three motorcycles."

24

Pick on Someone Else

Why doesn't General Motors give their
   Smogarian mechanics a coffee break?
It takes too long to retrain them.

❖ ❖ ❖

How many Smogarians does it take to change a
   light bulb?
Three. One to hold the bulb and two to turn the ladder.

❖ ❖ ❖

   "Do you speak Smogarian?"
   "No."
   "Do you read Smogarian?"
   "No."
   "Do you write Smogarian?"
   "No."
   "Do you know how many Smogarians are in
Smogaria?"

"No."

"How does it feel to be dumber than a Smogarian?"

✧ ✧ ✧

A perfect gift for a Smogarian who has everything . . . a garbage truck to keep it in.

✧ ✧ ✧

Did you know Smogarian dogs have flat noses . . . from chasing parked cars?

✧ ✧ ✧

Did you hear about the Smogarian race-track driver at Indianapolis who came in last? His average speed was 6.49 MPH. He had to make 75 pit stops—three for fuel, two to have the tires changed, and 70 to ask for directions.

✧ ✧ ✧

The most dangerous job in Smogaria?
Riding shotgun on a garbage truck.

✧ ✧ ✧

What's the capital of Smogaria?
About 13 dollars.

✧ ✧ ✧

Did you hear about the Smogarian beauty
    contest?
Nobody won.

✧ ✧ ✧

What's the difference between a Smogarian
    grandmother and an elephant?
About seven pounds.

✧ ✧ ✧

Why don't Smogarians kill flies?
The fly is their national bird.

✧ ✧ ✧

"Did you hear about the Smogarian orches-
tra that stopped in the middle of a performance
to clean the saliva out of their instruments?"
    "What's wrong with that?"
    "This was an all-string orchestra."

✧ ✧ ✧

Do you know why it takes a Smogarian five
    days to wash his basement windows?
*He needs four-and-a-half days to dig the holes for the
    ladder.*

25

Potluck

A man rose from his seat in a crowded bus so a lady standing nearby could sit down. She was so surprised she fainted.

When she revived and sat down, she said, "Thank you."

Then he fainted.

❖ ❖ ❖

Let me just say I've seen more excitement at the opening of an umbrella.

❖ ❖ ❖

What did the man say when he lost the fencing match?
Foiled again.

❖ ❖ ❖

Let me sum up this motion picture by saying I've seen better film on teeth!

❖ ❖ ❖

When an old TV star's show was canceled by the powers that be, a fan asked him, "Do you personally answer the hundreds of letters that come in every day demanding that your program be renewed?"

He answered disarmingly, "Goodness, no! I scarcely have time to write them!"

❖ ❖ ❖

The longest moment in the land of TV is the one that follows "We'll be right back."

❖ ❖ ❖

I once saw a movie that was so bad six states use it instead of capital punishment!

❖ ❖ ❖

I always do my exercises regularly in the morning. Immediately after waking I sternly say to myself, "Ready, now. Up. Down. Up. Down." And after two strenuous minutes I tell myself, "Okay, now try the other eyelid."

❖ ❖ ❖

A duck hunter, proud of his marksmanship, took his son out one morning to witness his skill. After some time a lone duck flew by.

"Watch this," whispered the dad, as he took careful aim and fired.

The duck flew serenely on.

"My boy," said the hunter, "you are witnessing a great miracle. There flies a dead duck."

❖ ❖ ❖

After a long evening of conversation the host said, "I hate to put you out, but I have to get up at six o'clock in the morning to catch a plane."

"Goodness gracious," exclaimed the guest, "I thought you were at my house!"

❖ ❖ ❖

Panting and perspiring, two men on a tandem bicycle at last got to the top of a steep hill.

"That was a stiff climb," said the first man.

"It certainly was," replied the second man. "And if I hadn't kept the brake on, we would have slid down backward."

❖ ❖ ❖

Some people are confirmed television addicts. I have a friend who turned on his radio the other night by mistake and thought he had gone blind.

✧ ✧ ✧

Don't be surprised if your next income tax form is simplified to contain only four lines:
What was your income last year?
What were your expenses?
How much do you have left?
Send it in.

✧ ✧ ✧

"My ancestry goes all the way back to Alexander the Great," one woman bragged. Then she turned to the woman on her left and asked, "And how far does your family go back?"

"I don't know," was the reply. "All of our records were lost in the Flood."

✧ ✧ ✧

Definition: Junk is the stuff we throw away; stuff is the junk we save.

✧ ✧ ✧

Nowadays a good conversationalist is anyone who can talk louder than the TV.

❖ ❖ ❖

Guest: What on earth do you put in your
     mattresses?
Innkeeper: The finest straw, sir.
Guest: Now I know where the straw that broke
     the camel's back came from.

❖ ❖ ❖

A man walked into the tax collector's office,
sat down, and smiled at everyone.

"May I help you?" asked the clerk in charge.

"No," said the man. "I just wanted to meet
the people I've been working for all these
years."

❖ ❖ ❖

The subject of my talk this afternoon is air
pollution . . . sometimes known as television.

❖ ❖ ❖

First actor: What's the matter with the leading
     lady?
Second actor: She only got nine bouquets of
     flowers tonight.
First actor: Good heavens! Isn't that enough?
Second actor: Nope. She paid for ten!

❖ ❖ ❖

A man walked by a table in a hotel and noticed three men and a dog playing cards. The dog was playing with extraordinary performance.

"This is a very smart dog," the man commented.

"Not so smart," said one of the players. "Every time he gets a good hand he wags his tail."

Two girls boarded a crowded bus and one of them whispered to the other: "Watch me embarrass a man into giving me his seat."

Pushing her way through the crowd, she turned all her charms upon a gentleman who looked like he might embarrass easily.

"My dear Mr. Wilson," she gushed, "fancy meeting you on the bus. Am I glad to see you. Why, you're almost a stranger. . . . My, but I'm tired."

The sedate gentleman looked up at the girl. He had never seen her before but he rose and said pleasantly, "Sit down, Mary, my girl. It isn't often I see you on washday. No wonder you're tired. Being pregnant isn't easy. By the way, don't deliver the wash until Thursday. My wife is going to the district attorney's office today to see if she can get your husband out of jail."

Teasers

How do you avoid falling hair?
Jump out of the way.

❖ ❖ ❖

You load 16 tons and what do you get?
A hernia.

❖ ❖ ❖

Name six animals that inhabit the Arctic region.
Three seals and three polar bears.

❖ ❖ ❖

Which month has 28 days?
They all do.

✧ ✧ ✧

Do you know what they got when they crossed
an abalone with a crocodile?
A crock-a-baloney!

✧ ✧ ✧

Do you know what they got when they crossed
a gorilla with a porcupine?
*I don't know what you call it, but it sure gets a seat
on the subway.*

✧ ✧ ✧

Do you know what they got when they crossed
a rattlesnake with a horse?
*I don't know what they called it, but if it bit you you
could ride it to the hospital.*

✧ ✧ ✧

What is practical nursing?
Falling in love with a rich patient!

✧ ✧ ✧

What do they call a German hippie?
A flowerkraut!

✧ ✧ ✧

Who invented the pendulum?
Pendulum Franklin.

❖ ❖ ❖

What weighs 2,500 pounds and wears flowers in
its hair?
A hippiepotamus.

❖ ❖ ❖

What do they call a man who steals ham?
A hamburglar.

❖ ❖ ❖

What's the best way to drive a baby buggy?
Tickle its feet.

❖ ❖ ❖

What would you get if you crossed a cow with a
porcupine?
A steak with a built-in toothpick.

❖ ❖ ❖

If a rooster laid an egg on the top of a hill, which
side would the egg roll down?
Neither side . . . a rooster can't lay eggs.

❖ ❖ ❖

Why does Santa Claus have three gardens?
So he can hoe, hoe, hoe.

❖ ❖ ❖

What animal can jump higher than a house?
Any animal . . . a house can't jump.

❖ ❖ ❖

What did the boy octopus say to the girl octopus?
I want to hold your hand hand hand hand hand hand hand hand.

❖ ❖ ❖

What did one casket say to the other casket?
Is that you, coffin?

❖ ❖ ❖

On which side does a chicken have the most feathers?
The outside.

❖ ❖ ❖

What's gray on the inside and clear on the outside?
An elephant in a baggie.

❖ ❖ ❖

What would you get if you crossed a flea with a rabbit?
A bug's bunny.

❖ ❖ ❖

Why do cows wear bells?
Because their horns don't work.

❖ ❖ ❖

What do you get when you cross a goat and an
owl?
A hootenanny.

❖ ❖ ❖

What do you get when you cross peanut butter
with an elephant?
*You either get peanut butter that never forgets or an
elephant that sticks to the roof of your mouth.*

❖ ❖ ❖

Why do elephants have wrinkles?
Have you ever tried to iron one?

❖ ❖ ❖

What do they call a bull that sleeps a lot?
A bulldozer.

❖ ❖ ❖

How many dead people are there in a cemetery?
All of them.

❖ ❖ ❖

What did one ear say to the other?
I didn't know we lived on the same block.

❖ ❖ ❖

Why did they make the fingers on the Statue of
Liberty only 11 inches long?
One inch longer and it would have been a foot.

✧ ✧ ✧

How do you make antifreeze?
Steal her blanket.

✧ ✧ ✧

April showers bring May flowers, but what do
Mayflowers bring?
Pilgrims.

✧ ✧ ✧

What does an elephant do when he hurts
his toe?
He calls a toe truck.

27

Working

An executive is a person who can take two hours for lunch without being missed.

✧ ✧ ✧

Employee: I have been here 11 years doing three men's work for one man's pay. Now I want a raise.
Boss: Well, I can't give you a raise, but if you'll tell me who the other two men are, I'll fire them.

✧ ✧ ✧

Employer: We can pay you 80 dollars a week now and 100 dollars a week in eight months.
Applicant: Thank you. I'll drop back in eight months.

❖ ❖ ❖

Worker: Boss, I came to see if you could raise my salary.

Boss: Relax and don't worry. I've managed to raise it each payday so far, haven't I?

❖ ❖ ❖

Every day Mr. Smith's secretary was 20 minutes late. Then one day she slid into place only five minutes tardy.

"Well," said Mr. Smith, "this is the earliest you've ever been late."

❖ ❖ ❖

An executive came home and slumped in his favorite chair with a discouraged look. His wife asked him what was wrong.

"You know those aptitude tests we're giving at the office? Well, I took one today for fun. It's a good thing I own the company."

❖ ❖ ❖

Boss: Jones, how long have you been working here?

Jones: Ever since I heard you coming down the hall.

❖ ❖ ❖

In a hat shop a saleslady gushed: "That's the hat for you. It makes you look ten years younger."

"Then I don't want it," retorted the customer. "I certainly can't afford to put on ten years every time I take off my hat!"

✧ ✧ ✧

Nobody is sicker than the man who is sick on his day off.

✧ ✧ ✧

A storekeeper stated in his will: "I want six of my creditors for pallbearers. . . . They have carried me so long they may as well finish the job."

✧ ✧ ✧

Boss: I notice you go out and get your hair cut during business hours.

Employee: My hair grows during business hours.

Boss: But it all doesn't grow during business hours.

Employee: I didn't get it all cut.

✧ ✧ ✧

Advertising manager: Where did you get this wonderful advertising idea? It would drag money out of anybody.

Assistant: I'll say it would. It's compiled from
the letters my daughter wrote me from
college.

✧ ✧ ✧

A salesman was assigned to secure an important client but failed in his mission. He faxed his
secretary and asked her to break the news indi-
rectly to his boss. His note read, "Failed in secur-
ing client, prepare the boss."

He received the following fax from his secretary: "The boss is prepared . . . prepare yourself."

Other Books by Bob Phillips